Knitting Woolscapes

Designs Inspired by Coastal Marin Wool

Marlie de Swart

Knitting Woolscapes

Like landscapes, woolscapes offer visual and sensory experiences that are unique to a specific geography. Rolling hills of pastures dotted with sheep and cows and edged by the Pacific Ocean, define the essence of Coastal Marin in Northern California. The handmade designs with local wool and fiber from this "terroir" offer fashionable, long-wearing garments that are in harmony with the landscape.

Knitting Woolscapes

Designs Inspired by Coastal Marin Wool

Marlie de Swart

Photography: Paige Green

Text: Marlie de Swart
Photography: Paige Green
(except for back ground images and images on pages 7, 8, 9,
30, 31, 33, 113 which are by the author)
Book and Page Design: Susie Pinkerton

Published in the United States in 2016.

Library of Congress Catalog-in-Publication Data
de Swart, Marlie, 2016
Knitting Woolscapes: Designs Inspired by Coastal Marin Wool
ISBN 978-0-692-74293-8
1. Knitting Patterns. 2. Wool.

Printed in the USA

CONTENTS

CONTENTS continued

. . . .

Color Section - Gallery
Hand-spun, hand-dyed, color-carded and color-plyed:
All the wool, alpaca and angora rabbit is local, and the roving was dyed with
commercially available green acid dyes.

Foreword

This book was created from a desire to knit with local yarns. When I first began knitting in West Marin, not many local yarns were available. Since I was a spinner as well as a knitter, it was only natural to make my own yarns and to knit with the available fibers from local farmers.

Many farms in rural West Marin have sheep and alpacas (fiber animals) in addition to vegetables and cattle. The farms with one or two pet sheep or alpacas don't quite know what to do with their fleeces. So they come by my store, Black Mountain Artisans, which is a fiber artists' collective in downtown Point Reyes Station, California, and give or sell these fleeces to us.

My very first fleeces in West Marin, many years ago, were from Doris Ober and Richard Kirschman of Dogtown, just a few miles north of Bolinas where I live. They had five Jacob sheep and gave me their fleeces every year. Now, twenty years later with all their animals passed on, they asked me to make them something from the fleece of Quentin, their last llama who died recently.

The yarns of West Marin reflect their coastal environment which is foggy and damp to semi-arid in a somewhat rugged setting. Most yarns are rustic and fall within a middle range of softness and coarseness. Mixing the fleeces of these breeds of sheep with Alpaca renders a shiny and soft yet rustic yarn. This is reflected in the designs of the garments in this book.

Over the past ten years a shift has occurred, and many of the lands in rural West Marin have turned into boutique farms with people developing their own expensive yarn brands. Every year I choose a small number of sheep fleeces and alpaca blankets and have them processed at Yolo Wool Mill in Yolo County, some eighty miles northeast of San Francisco. I make sure I have enough to create my samples and for some D.I.Y. kits. At the end of the book is a list of my fiber sources.

Acknowledgements

All the patterns in this book were test knitted, most of them by a Bolinas friend and fellow knitter, Barbara MacDonald.

Having your garments "test" knitted is the best way to learn how you work. It also teaches you how to write patterns. It tells you whether you are a loose or a tight knitter. (I am a loose knitter.) It illustrates what you take for granted and what you assume other people know. It is one thing to knit for pleasure and improvise as you create. It is an entirely different thing to knit while writing instructions for another knitter.

When I create a garment, I first look at the yarn. The yarn dictates whether it should be a sweater or a scarf, worn next to the skin or over something else. Sometimes I do a little drawing to explore the overall design and the texture of the garment. Then I start knitting, usually the back panel first. When I am half-way through, I sometimes turn it upside down or sideways to see whether a different way of looking at it will change my design.

These patterns wouldn't be publishable if it were not for Barbara's conscientious efforts in knitting and re-knitting, writing and re-writing and asking questions. In some cases she knit one garment seven times, as in the case of the Milk Maid Top, just to get the rib pattern perfectly merged in the front and the back. A "thank-you" goes to Heidi Tumerman, Sophie Dawson and Charmaine Krieger, three other test knitters and Sue Buster for meticulously proofreading all the patterns.

Photographer Paige Green showed off the garments at their best. Doing a photoshoot with her is like a ballet. The photographer moves as the principal dancer surrounded by the stylist, the photo assistant, the hair stylist and the models. Everyone and everything is in flux and going in and out of focus. In our one-and-a-half-day long photoshoot we moved around the beaches and town of Bolinas with all the people and entourage in constant motion and preparedness.

A special thank-you to Laura Schneider, Paige's assistant and model; Tessa Watson, stylist; Sara Landa, hair stylist; Emi Lovemelipe, Valerie Yep, Jeannie Phan, Ashley Brock, Vanessa Wering, and Allison Arnold, models. And a special thanks to my husband Bruce who was there carrying and ferrying everything, enabling the day-and-a-half long process and who has seen me through the rest of this project.

Introduction

I was raised in Holland. Two of my aunts were Franciscan nuns. They taught "Fiber Works" sewing - knitting - embroidering etc. to high schoolers. It was inevitable that I learned to knit at an early age; even my brothers learned to knit. When I was seven, my family moved to a small village (a parish really) just outside of Breda in Southern Holland. The community consisted mostly of rural, small subsistence farmers who had a few cows, pigs, some sheep, vicious watch dogs and small parcels of land for crops that they sold.

One such farmer's family had a thirty-something developmentally disabled daughter who knit quite well. For a while she knit the underwear for my siblings and me in white cotton. My mother insisted on helping this farmer's family by purchasing these unfashionable, too large garments.

Much later when I was living in Amsterdam, I got in touch with a family friend who lived in a nearby village, close to the dikes. Dikes are perfect for grazing sheep since they don't sink into the mud as cows would. This friend supplied me with six or seven fleeces a year, which I spun mostly in worsted singles. I filled my ten square feet project room from top to bottom with hand-spun yarn and hand-knit sweaters which I sold or gave away before returning to the U. S. Even then, people loved the local hand-spun wool and the characteristic garments they inspired.

After moving back to San Francisco and working in Silicon Valley for a while, I retired to Coastal Marin and took over Black Mountain Weavers/Artisans and started to create yarns again under the brand name Bo-Rage Yarns.

This book is arranged in three sections. The first two parts are dedicated to patterns made with natural colored local wool, focusing on construction and texture and closely related to the local landscape. All these garments fit within the parameters set by Fibershed.

The third "color" section has patterns from home processed and hand-spun local wool, dyed with commercially available dyes.

The patterns are rated for skill levels.
Easy - means you know the basic stitches and minimal shaping.
Intermediate - assumes you have some knitting experience and know more intricate stitches, shaping and finishing.
Experienced - means you can work with more complicated shaping and finishing.

PART ONE

NATURAL COLORED GARMENTS

Structural Elements

Fibershed's parameters are: local fiber, local dye and local labor

I encountered Fibershed in West Marin in recent years when it first started. It was only natural that I became part of this movement. It has been very exciting and gratifying to see how this concept of local fiber, local dye and local labor, started by a younger generation, has evolved and spread through the U.S. and beyond.

All the garments in these first 2 sections are within the parameters of Fibershed. I have used the natural colors of the sheep. The yarns are mill-spun, except for one or two garments, which are hand-spun.

The first focus in the natural color section is on the construction of the garments. These garments are not straightforward. In all cases they are knit in panels or parts that are sewn together afterwards. Often the shaping of the sleeves or fronts is achieved by means of short rows. Some garments are knit in identical panels and some are knit from top to bottom to get the right flair and front closure. Most garments in this book are written for a medium-sized person.

Every year I select a small number of fleeces from local sheep, alpacas, angora goats and rabbits. I mix these fibers for color and softness and have them milled at Yolo Woolen Mill for Bo-Rage mill-spun yarn.

I have indicated the yarn equivalent in commercially available yarns where appropriate, not only to compare the yarn gauge but also to offer yarn alternatives.

Milk Maid Top

The bodice of a typical old Dutch peasant costume was shaped close to the body, bust and waist and usually worn with wide skirts, black stockings and wooden shoes.   This inspired me to make this Milk Maid Top from Bo-Rage mill-spun soft grey wool and alpaca. The distinctive shape of this bodice is achieved through stitch reduction in the front and back panels. The shape of the shoulders and sleeves is created by means of short rows.

Skill level:
Intermediate to experienced

Measurements:
The size given fits a small to medium size person and may look best on someone that size. Only one size is given.

Finished size:
Top to bottom: 17"
Bottom to under arm sleeve: 5"
Bottom width: 14"
Top width (inc. sleeves) 29"

Yarn:
Bo-Rage mill-spun 2 ply. Heavy worsted yarn, approx. 800 yards

Commercial yarn equivalent is Brown Sheep Lamb's Pride worsted weight

Needles:
Circular or straight #8 or size to obtain gauge. Main needle
Circular 24" #6 needle or two sizes below main needle

Notions:
Four long stitch holders (optional)
Tapestry needle
Stitch markers

Gauge:
4sts. = 1 inch
5.5 rows = 1 inch

General note:
Structurally the sweater is made up of the front and back panels. The sleeves/shoulders are formed by picking up stitches along the sides of front and back panels and then using short rows and the Wrap and Turn (W&T) technique to create the distinctive shoulder curve.

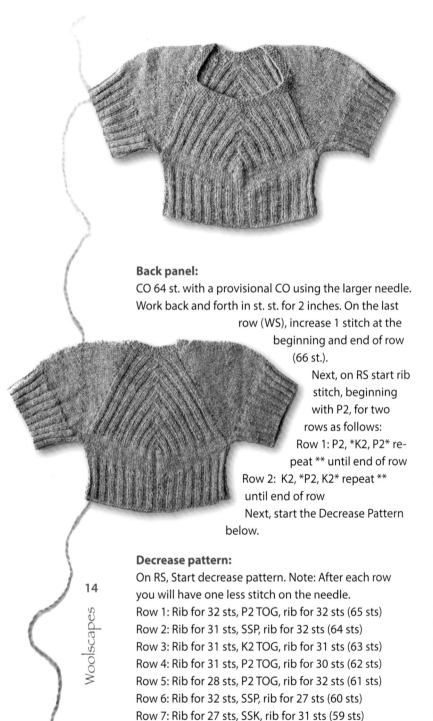

Back panel:

CO 64 st. with a provisional CO using the larger needle. Work back and forth in st. st. for 2 inches. On the last row (WS), increase 1 stitch at the beginning and end of row (66 st.).

Next, on RS start rib stitch, beginning with P2, for two rows as follows:

Row 1: P2, *K2, P2* repeat ** until end of row

Row 2: K2, *P2, K2* repeat ** until end of row

Next, start the Decrease Pattern below.

Decrease pattern:

On RS, Start decrease pattern. Note: After each row you will have one less stitch on the needle.

Row 1: Rib for 32 sts, P2 TOG, rib for 32 sts (65 sts)
Row 2: Rib for 31 sts, SSP, rib for 32 sts (64 sts)
Row 3: Rib for 31 sts, K2 TOG, rib for 31 sts (63 sts)
Row 4: Rib for 31 sts, P2 TOG, rib for 30 sts (62 sts)
Row 5: Rib for 28 sts, P2 TOG, rib for 32 sts (61 sts)
Row 6: Rib for 32 sts, SSP, rib for 27 sts (60 sts)
Row 7: Rib for 27 sts, SSK, rib for 31 sts (59 sts)
Row 8: Rib for 30 sts, SSP, rib for 27 sts (58 sts)

Row 9: Rib for 28 str, P2 TOG, rib for 28 sts (57 sts)
Row 10: Rib for 27 sts, P2 TOG, rib for 28 sts (56 sts)
Row 11: Rib for 27 sts, K2 TOG, rib for 27 sts (55 sts)
Row 12: Rib for 27 sts, P2 TOG, rib for 26 sts (54 sts)
Row 13: Rib for 25 sts, K2 TOG, rib for 27 sts (53 sts)
Row 14: Rib for 27 sts, P2 TOG, rib for 24 sts (52 sts)
Row 15: Rib for 23 sts, SSK, rib for 27 sts (51 sts)
Row 16: Rib for 26 sts, SSP, rib for 23 sts (50 sts)
Row 17: Rib for 23 sts, SSK, rib for 25 sts (49 sts)
Row 18: Rib for 23 sts, SSP, rib for 24 sts (48 sts)
Row 19: Rib for 23 sts, SSK, rib for 23 sts (47 sts)
Row 20: Rib for 23 sts, P2 TOG, rib for 22 sts (46 sts)
Row 21: Rib for 20 sts, SSP, rib for 24 sts (45 sts)
Row 22: Rib for 23 sts, P2 TOG, rib for 20 sts (44 sts)
Row 23: Rib for 19 sts, SSK, rib for 23 sts (43 sts)
Row 24: Rib for 22 sts, SSP, rib for 19 sts (42 sts)
Row 25: Rib for 20 sts, P2 TOG, rib for 20 sts (41 sts)
Row 26: Rib for 20 sts, SSP, rib for 19 sts (40 sts)
Row 27: Rib for 19 sts, K2 TOG, rib for 19 sts (39 sts)
Row 28: Rib for 19 sts, P2 TOG, rib for 18 sts (38 sts)
Row 29: Rib for 16 sts, P2 TOG, rib for 20 sts (37 sts)
Row 30: Rib for 20 sts, SSP, rib for 15 sts (36 sts)
Row 31: Rib for 15 sts, SSK, rib for 19 sts (35 sts)
Row 32: Rib for 18 sts, SSP, rib for 15 sts (34 sts)
Row 33: Rib for 16 sts, P2 TOG, rib for 16 sts (33 sts)
Row 34: Rib for 15 sts, P2 TOG, rib for 16 sts (32 sts)
Row 35: Rib for 15 sts, K2 TOG, rib for 15 sts (31 sts)
Row 36: Rib for 15 sts, P2 TOG, rib for 14 sts (30 sts)
Row 37: Rib for 13 sts, K2 TOG, rib for 15 sts (29 sts)
Row 38: Rib for 15 sts, P2 TOG, rib for 12 sts (28 sts)
Row 39: Rib for 11 sts, SSK, rib for 15 sts (27 sts)
Row 40: Rib for 14 sts, SSP, rib for 11 sts (26 sts)
Row 41: Rib for 11 sts, SSK, rib for 13 sts (25 sts)
Row 42: Rib for 12 sts, SSP, rib for 11 sts (24 sts)
Row 43: Rib for 11 sts, K2 TOG, rib for 11 sts (23 sts)
Row 44: Rib for 11 sts, P2 TOG, rib for 10 sts (22 sts)
Row 45: Rib for 9 sts, P2 TOG, rib for 11 sts (21 sts)
Row 46: Rib for 12 sts, SSP, rib for 7 sts (20 sts)
Row 47: Rib for 7 sts, SSK, rib for 11 sts (19 sts)
Row 48: Rib for 10 sts, SSP, rib for 7 sts (18 sts)
Row 49: Rib for 8 sts, P2 TOG, rib for 8 sts (17 sts)

Row 50: Rib for 7 sts, P2 TOG, rib for 8 sts (16 sts)
Row 51: Rib for 7 sts, K2 TOG, rib for 7 sts (15 sts)
Row 52: Rib for 7 sts, P2 TOG, rib for 6 sts (14 sts)
Bind off provisionally.

Front panel:
Cast on 64 with provisional CO.
Follow instructions for back panel until you start the decrease pattern.
Next, start the decrease pattern.

Decrease pattern:
On RS, start decreases as follows:
Rows 1-28: Follow instruction for back panel. You should now have 38 sts on needle.
Place the 38 sts on a holder or do a provisional bind off.

Back right sleeve/shoulder:
With RS of back panel facing you, and top to your right, PU 40 sts.
Purl one row on WS and knit one row on RS. Next, starting on the WS begin the sleeve/shoulder using short rows (W&T).
Row 1: P 2 sts, W&T
Row 2: RS - Knit back to end of row (will be back to top of panel). This is repeated after every W&T row
Rows 3: P 5 sts, W&T
Row 4: and all WS rows, Repeat row 2
Row 5: P 8 sts, W&T
Row 7: P 11 sts, W&T
Row 9: P 14 sts, W&T
Row 11: P 17 sts, W&T
Row 13: P 20 sts, W&T
Row 15: P 23 sts, W&T
Row 17: P 26 sts, W&T
Row 19: P 29 sts, W&T
Row 21: P 32 sts, W&T
Row 23: P 35 sts W&T
Row 25: P 38 sts, W&T
Row 26: Repeat row 2
Half the sleeve/shoulder is done and you can see the curve.

Repeat Rows 1-26
Then, purl one row and knit one row.
Put these 40 sts on holder or do provisional bind off.

Back left sleeve/shoulder:
With RS of back panel facing and top to your left, PU 40 sts.
Purl one row on WS. Next, on RS, begin short rows.
Row 1: K 2 sts, W&T
Row 2: WS - Purl back to beg. of row (you will be back at top of panel). This is repeated after every W&T row.
Rows 3: K 5 sts, W&T
Row 4: and all WS rows, Repeat row 2.
Row 5: K 8 sts, W&T
Row 7: K 11 sts, W&T
Row 9: K 14 sts, W&T
Row 11: K 17 sts, W&T
Row 13: K 20 sts, W&T
Row 15: K 23 sts, W&T
Row 17: K 26 sts, W&T
Row 19: K 29 sts, W&T
Row 21: K 32 sts, W&T
Row 23: K 35 sts, W&T
Row 25: K 39 sts, W&T
Row 26: Repeat row 2
Repeat Rows 1-26.
Next, purl one row and knit one row.
Put the 40 sts on holder or bind off provisionally.

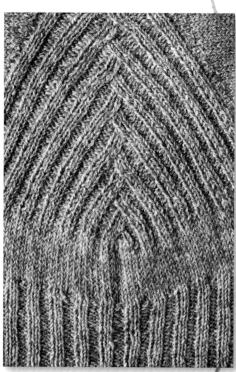

Front right sleeve/shoulder:
With RS of front facing you and top of panel to your right, PU 24 stitches. Knit a row on RS and purl a row on WS. Next, cast on 16 stitches at top of panel, using the knitted cast on method. There are now 40 sts on needle.

This will be your right shoulder and neckline.

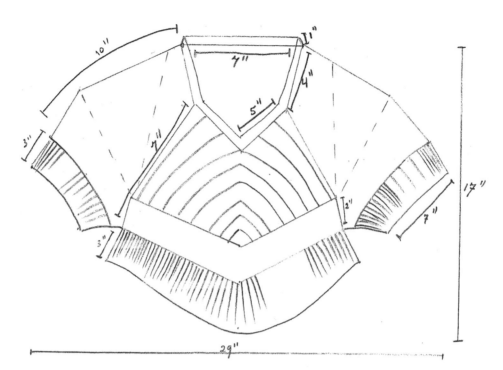

With the RS facing knit one row and purl one row.

Next, start sleeve/shoulder with short rows (RS facing, top to right) as follows:

Row 1: K 2 sts, W&T

Row 2: Purl back to beg. of row (top of panel). This is repeated after every Wrap and Turn row.

Rows 3: K 5 sts, W&T

Row 4: and all WS rows: Repeat row 2.

Row 5: K 8 sts, W&T

Row 7: K 11 sts, W&T

Row 9: K 14 sts, W&T

Row 11: K 17 sts, W&T

Row 13: K 20 sts, W&T

Row 15: K 23 sts, W&T

Row: 17: K 26 sts, W&T

Row 19: K 29 sts, W&T

Row 21: K 32 sts, W&T

Row 23: K 35 sts, W&T

Row 25: K 38 sts, W&T

Row 26: Repeat row 2.

Repeat rows 1-26.

Then, knit one row and purl one row.

Put 40 sts on a holder or do a provisional bind off.

Left front sleeve/shoulder:

With the RS of front panel facing you and the top of panel to your left, PU 24 stitches.

With RS facing, knit one row.

Next cast on 16 sts at top of panel using the knitted CO method. There are now 40 sts on the needle. Next start left shoulder with short rows using the W&T method. Starting with the WS facing, and panel top to your right, begin the W&T method as follows:

Row 1: P 2, W&T

Row 2: RS - Knit back to end of row. You will now be back at the panel top. This is repeated after every W&T row.

Rows 3: P 5, W&T

Row 4 and all WS rows: Repeat row 2.

Row 5: P 8, W&T

Row 7: P 11, W&T

Row 8: P 14, W&T
Row 9: P 17, W&T
Row 11: P 20, W&T
Row 13: P 23, W&T
Row 15: P 26, W&T
Row 17: P 29, W&T
Row 19: P 32, W&T
Row 20: Repeat row 2.
Repeat rows 1-21.
Purl one row
Knit one row
Put the 40 sts stitches on a holder or bind off provisionally.

Bottom ribbing:
At the bottom of the sweater, transfer the provisional stitches onto the 24" smaller circular needle, 128 sts., and work in rib pattern for 3.5 inches.
Bind off loosely in pattern.

Sleeve ribbing:
Transfer the 80 sts. from the two holders to the smaller 16# inch circular needle. Work in rib pattern for 3.5 inches. Bind off loosely in pattern.

Neck:
PU 100 stitches on the smaller 24" circular needle. With RS facing and starting at right back neck, PU 18 sts on the back of the neck, PU 22 sts on left side of neck, PU 38 sts on the front of the neck, and 22 sts on the right side of the neck for 100 sts. PM
Knit in seed stitch for 1". Bind off loosely.
Weave in all loose ends.
Block sweater by washing; press out water with a towel; block to size and shape desired.

Instructions for special techniques:
Working short rows:
First work up to the place where you will begin your short rows. Note that in this pattern, the Left Back Sleeve/Shoulder and the Right Front Sleeve/Shoulder short rows are done with the RS facing while, the Right Back/Shoulder and the Left Front Sleeve/Shoulder short rows are done with the WS facing.
In the pattern directions, these six steps are referred to as "W&T". RS short rows:
Step 1: With the yarn in back, slip the next stitch purl-wise.
Step 2: Bring the yarn between the needles to the front.
Step 3: Slip the same stitch back to the left-hand needle.
Step 4: Turn the work around and bring the yarn to the purl side between the needles. One stitch is wrapped.
Step 5: Purl all stitches on left needle.
Step 6: Turn the work back to the right side where you will perform the next short row.

WS Short Rows:
Step 1: With the yarn in back, slip the next stitch purl-wise.
Step 2: Bring the yarn between the needles to the front.
Step 3: Slip the same stitch back to the left-hand needle.
Step 4: Turn the work around and bring the yarn to the knit side between the needles. One stitch is wrapped.
Step 5: Knit all stitches on left needle.
Step 6: Turn the work back to the WS where you will perform the next short row.

The wrap & turn short row method leaves a decorative ridge on the sleeve.

Leaf Hat

This hat consists of four large leaves. These leaves are pointed at the top and rounded at the bottom with a fatter middle, the same shape as a crown or a hat. The size of the hat can be changed by making the leaves smaller or larger, which can be done by using thinner or larger yarn and needles.

Skill level:
Intermediate

Finished size:
1 leaf is 10" long and 7" at the widest part.

Yarn:
One skein (200 yards of heavy worsted wool) Bo-Rage mill-spun
Equivalent commercial weight yarn is Brown Sheep, Lamb's Pride worsted weight

Needles:
24" circular #8 needle or needle size to obtain gauge. Main needle
24" circular #6 needle for the band or two sizes below main needle.

Notions:
Tapestry needle

Gauge:
4 st = 1inch
5.5 rows = 1inch

General note:
You create four large leaves. You knit the leaves separately and then sew them together. Sew the top (up to 1.5" from the bottom of the leaf) together to form the crown/bowl of the hat. Then you pick up stitches 1.5" from the bottom and create the head band.

Leaf:
Cast on 9 st.

Knit and purl first 2 rows.
Row 3: K4, YO, K1, YO, K4
Row 4: and all even rows: Purl.
Row 5: K5, YO, K1, YO, K5.
Row 7: K6 YO, K1, YO, K6.
Row 9: K7, YO, K1, YO, K7.
Continue until you have 33 stitches
Knit next row.
Purl next row.
Now your decreases start.
Next row: K2 TOG, K15, slip 1, K16.
Next row: P2 TOG, and P to end of row.
Next row: K2 TOG, K14, slip 1, K15.
Next row: P2 TOG, P to end of row.
Repeat these last 2 rows in which you reduce 1 st. each row, until you have one stitch left. Pull yarn through loop.

Repeat this leaf 3 more times.

Block all the leaves so they lay flat and will be easier to sew together. Sew the top of the leaves together in such a way that the seam becomes part of the design. Sew them together up to about 1.5" from the bottom edge.

Head band:
Pick up 68 stitches approx. 1.5" from the bottom of the leaves on the WS (purl side) of the leaf (see picture). Knit the band down. The bottom part of the leaves will create a crown effect as they curl up.

With needle size #6, with the RS facing you.
Row 1: K
Row 2: Start rib pattern (K2, P2).
Cont. in rib pattern for 3 inches.
Bind off.

Finishing:
Weave in all loose ends.

This shows where to pick up the stitches to start the hat band. Pick up on the WS (purl side) of the leaf.

Woolscapes

The Estero Vest

The multiple waterways of the Estero in the Point Reyes National Seashore snake inland through deep canyons that have open, exposed pasture land on the bluffs. The ribbed texture of this vest flows from the back over the shoulders to the front to form the basic outline of the vest, similar to the flow of the Estero.

Skill:
Intermediate

Measurements:
One size is given. The sample fits a medium to large person. Using smaller or larger needles and thinner or thicker yarn will result in a different sizes.

Finished size:
Total length 23"
Bottom to armhole 11"

Yarn:
Color 1: as shown, natural white, bulky, single, 3 skeins or approx. 600 yards, 12oz.
Color 2: as shown. natural grey. Bo-Rage mill-spun Shetland Tweed. 1 skein approx. 200 yards, 4 oz.
Other sample shows Bo-Rage mill-spun, indigo dyed, heavy worsted weight, 2 ply.

Commercial yarn equivalent is Imperial Yarn Erin, heavy worsted weight.

Needles:
#10 circular needle or size to obtain gauge. Main needle

Notions:
Tapestry needle
Tape measure

Gauge:
3 st. = 1 inch
5 rows = 1 inch

General note:
This pattern is knit in sections. You start with the back panel which has increases up the center of the back to shape from the waist (narrow) to the shoulders (broader) and then travels over the shoulders to form the fronts. Then stitches are picked up along the side of the back panel to create the side panels. The side panels are shaped in such a way as to make the front swing upwards. Then stitches are picked up along the front panels to create the collar. Stitches are picked up again from the side panel under the arm to create a grey visible gusset, the arm hole band and the cap sleeves.

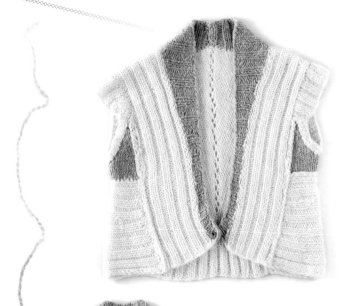

middle of the panel and form a nice pattern.

Next row: (row 23) work in pattern for 16 st., P3, YO, P3, (to create a hole and increase a stitch) and work in pattern to the end of the row.
Next row: work in pattern.
Next row: (row 25) work in pattern for 16 st., P4, YO, P3, work in pattern to end of row.
Next row: work in pattern.
Next row (row 27) work in pattern for 16 st., P4, YO, P4, work in pattern to end of row.
Next row: work in pattern.
Next row: (row 29) work in pattern for 16 st. P5, YO, P4, work in pattern to end of row.
Continue in this manner until you have 16" inches from the bottom.

When you reach 16" from the bottom (62 st.), you will reduce 1st of the center purl section, each side, every 4 rows over the next 4 inches. Reduce these stitches after you knit and purl the ribs, where the purl section starts and again before the ribs start. As follows:
Next row: (*)work in rib pattern, (3X all the ribs), P2 TOG, P the purl section, while keeping the central YO increase, then SSK, the last 2 st. on the purl central section before the ribbing starts, work in rib pattern, (3X all the ribs).
Next row: work in pattern(*)

Repeat these 2 rows, 2 more times.

When you reach 20" from the bottom, you should have 58 stitches at the top.

Next you start on the front panels.
Knit 16 st. in pattern and put the remaining st. on a stitch holder. These 16 stitches become your right or left front panel.

Front panels:
The front panels should be approx. 19" long from the shoulder.

Back panel:
Cast on 38 stitches with C1
Rib Stitch pattern is K2 P2
RS: *K2, P2* repeat, end with K2
WS: *P2, K2* repeat, end with P2
Work in pattern for 12 rows, 3 inches, then break the pattern lines. Instead of K2, P2. work P2 ,K2, for 2 rows, then back again to K2, P2 pattern for 1.5" more inches or 6 rows until you reach 4.5 inches.
This is where you begin to shape the back.
Place a stitch marker at the center of the panel (the 19th st.).
Next row: (row 21) work in pattern for 18 st., then p 6 st. (center st.) and continue in pattern to the end of the row.
Next row: work in pattern, knit the 6 center sts.
At this point you will start to increase a stitch every other row with a Yarn Over at the center of the panel.
In the picture you can see that the YO is one stitch after or before the previous YO, so the holes stay in the

Woolscapes

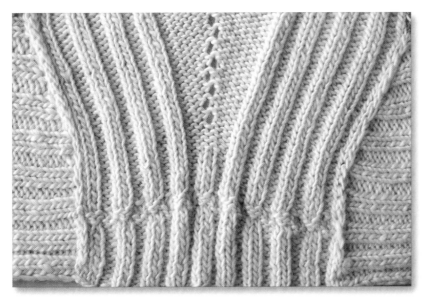

the bottom of the vest and 5" at the arm opening.

Do the same on the other side making sure that the bottom of the vest has the increases. Sew the side panels to the fronts. You will have a large arm opening. This is where the gusset will go.

Gusset: (underarm)
You are working below the right arm opening with the right side of the garment facing you. Pick up 16 stitches with (C2) the grey yarn. Knit and purl 6 rows (stocki-

Continue knitting (16 st.) in rib pattern. Work in pattern until you reach19" from the shoulder. Bind off. Do the same for the other side. Leave the center 26 stitches of the back on a stitch holder.

Side panels:
These are made with short rows with a circular needle. Don't knit in a circle but back and forth. Pick up the stitches without knitting them.   Only knit them after all the st. are on the needle.

Pick up stitches from the back panel, 34 st. over 9" from the bottom up. With the right side of the knitting facing you and the bottom of the back panel on your right hand side, pick up 34 st. from the side bottom part of the back panel. You will have 34 st. on your needle. Knit short rows from the bottom up.

Knit the first 2 stitches, turn and purl back.
Next row: K2, P2 (4 stitches) Turn, K2 and P2.
Next row: K2, P2, K2 (6 st.) Turn, P2, K2, P2
Continue in this manner until you have knit and purled all 34 stitches on your left needle. Now continue in rib pattern for 5" or approx. 20 rows.
Bind off. The side panel should measure approx. 11" on

Now repeat the process for the other side.
Pick up the sts. from the stitch holder.
K to end of row, pick up 1 st. from side.
Turn, Purl picked up st. and first st. together, and P to end of row.
K2 TOG, K to end of row. Repeat these 2 rows until there are no st. left.
Do the other arm opening gusset the same way.

Sleeve cap:

With (C1) the white wool, pick up 58 st. around the whole arm opening starting and stopping at the bottom of the armhole. Work in rib pattern (K2, P2). You don't work this in the round, but straight.
In rib pattern (K2, P2) work 3 rows.
Next row – *bind off 14 st., knit in pattern to end of row*.
Next row – repeat previous row. Only the top of the sleeve will be worked further.
Next row – *bind off 2 st., knit in pattern to end of row*.
Next rows – repeat previous row 3 more times.
Bind off.
Sew bottom end of the arm opening together.
Do the other arm opening the same way.

Collar:

The collar is knit from the corner where the front panel and the back panel meet. As you work in rib pattern (K2, P2) pick up 2 stitches on each side, both sides (4 st. all together), 2 st. from the back panel and 2 st. from the front panel. It is knit in two sections that meet at the center of the back and are sewn together after you are finished.

With (C2), the grey wool, pick up 2 st. at the corner of back panel and front panel. Work in rib pattern (K2, P2). Increase (pick up) 2 st. on each side until you reach the center of the back. (13 st. each side of the corner, 26 st. on your needle and about 14 rows) Stop increasing at the center of the back, but continue with the

nette stitch) while picking up stitches along the side.
K first st and picked up st. together. (Make sure not to increase the stitch count.)
After 6 rows, place a marker in the center.
You are creating a V shape for the arm opening
Row 7: Knit to center.
Row 8: Turn, bind off one stitch (or K2 TOG) and purl back.
(Put the stitches for the other side on a stitch holder.)
Continue in this manner, knitting the first st and picked up st. on the side together, and P2 TOG at the center, until you have no stitches left, approx. 5" along the front side.

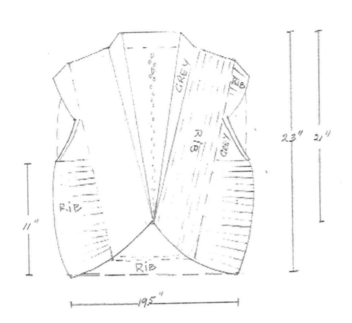

2 st. increase on the front side of the vest until you are about 10" from the bottom of the vest. Then pick up all the stitches to the bottom edge of the vest. You now should have 64 st. on your needle. Knit 4 more rows in rib pattern until you have a total of 24 rows at the deepest point (the corner of the front and back panels) and 4 rows at the bottom of the vest.
Bind off.
Do the same for the other side.

Finishing:
Sew the back of the collar together. Weave in all the loose strands and gently block the vest.

A gusset was originally designed to afford more arm movement in tight knitted sweaters.

Pinwheel Beret

FROM A SAMPLING OF BO-RAGE MILL-SPUN YARNS

The top of this beret is knit in eight sections. Each section is a triangle knit by means of short rows*. When you finish one section, you change color and start with the next one until you have all eight sections. Then you sew together the last and the first section to create the circle. The band is knit after you finish the circle top by picking up stitches along the outer edge.

Skill level:
Easy

Finished size:
11" diameter

Yarn:
Part skeins of Bo-Rage mill-spun yarn, heavy worsted, 2 ply
In the sample I used approx. 250 yards total.
Each section uses approx. 25 yards plus the band.

Needles:
#8 24" circular needle or needle size to obtain gauge. Main needle
#6 (or 2 sizes smaller than the main needle) for the head band

Notions:
Tapestry needle
Stitch marker

Gauge:
4 st. = 1 inch
5 rows = 1 inch

First Section of the top of the beret:
With needle size #8 CO 26 stitches

Row 1: Knit
Row 2: Purl (and all even rows).
Row 3: Bind off 2 stitches at the beginning of every knit row, so every 2 rows.
Row 4: Purl
Repeat rows 3 and 4 until you have 2 stitches left.
Next: Pick up 24 stitches along the long side (or the hypotenuse) of the triangle (26 st.)
With a different color, repeat the directions for the previous section. Do this a total of eight times. Sew the first and the last sections into a flat circle.

Beret band:
With needle size #6 and the right side facing you, pick up 104 stitches along the outer edge of the circle. Place a marker at the beginning of the row.
With the RS facing you knit 1 row.
Work rib pattern (K2, P2) for 4 rows.
Row 6: K2 TOG every 6 stitches as follows: K2, P2, K2, P2 TOG. (91 st.)
Repeat the decreases to end of row.
Row 7: Knit and purl in pattern.
Row 8: Decrease 1 st. every 5 st. as follows: K2, P2tog, K2, P1. (73 st.)
Knit and purl in pattern for 5 more rows without decreasing.
Bind off.

Finishing:
Weave in all loose ends and gently press the beret in shape.

* Short Row Explanation:
Begin the row on RS.
Bind off 2 st. knit to end of row.
Turn work and purl to end of row.
Repeat until 2 st. are left.

Structural Elements

Stinson Shrug

This shrug happened when I was trying to make a shawl with my hand-spun yarns. I was knitting along and decided that this shawl would look great as a shrug. So, I added the back portion. The construction is very easy to make: just one large rectangle and a square for the back panel.

Skill level:
Intermediate

Measurements:
The sample is for a medium to large person. Sizes can be changed by using thicker wool and larger needles or thinner wool and smaller needles.
For a child's version, see end of the pattern.

Finished size:
Length, bottom to shoulder: 20"
Front panel width: 11" each
Back panel: 14.5" long and 17" wide

Yarn:
This pattern can be made with any colored yarn. In the sample, all the yarns are a similar worsted weight. The following yarns were used:
1 skein of light brown Bo-Rage mill-spun 2 ply, worsted weight, 200 yards, 4 oz.

1/2 skein of Bo-Rage mill-spun 2 ply, white, approx. 100 yards, 2 oz.
1/2 skein of Bo-Rage mill-spun, 2 ply, grey, approx. 100 yards, 2 oz.
1 skein of Bo-Rage hand-spun 2 ply, black, divided into 3 equal balls to use as the bottom part of the fronts and back, approx. 200 yards, 4 oz.
Various very small amounts of other colors
C1 – Dark Brown/Black Divided into 3 equal parts
C2 – Dark Gray
C3 – Tan /Light Brown
C4 – Crème/Off White
C5 – Light Gray
Commercial available equivalent yarns are Brown Sheep, Lamb's Pride worsted weight.

Needles:
US size #6 or size needle to obtain the desired gauge.
Main needle

Notions:
Embroidery needle
Stitch markers
Measuring tape

Structural Elements

Gauge:
4.5 st. = 1 inch
6 rows = 1 inch

General note:
This shrug is made in two pieces. The first piece is knit in one long strip (approx. 55" long X 11" wide) and constitutes the right front, shoulders, upper back, and left front. The second piece is a square that is added to create the lower back.

The whole garment is knit in garter stitch meaning all rows are knit. Small square inserts are added for interest and contrast and require knowledge of two color knitting, carrying colors on the wrong side of the knitted piece and using purl stitch on the wrong side of the inserted section. If unfamiliar with two color knitting, sometimes referred to as "stranding," refer to instructions on the internet or instructional book. Refer to illustrations to check measurements of sections as they are knit. Directions for making a child's version are at the end of the pattern.

Right front:
Begin with bottom right front point:
Using C1, cast on 5 sts. Knitting all rows (garter stitch), increase 1 st. (kfb) at the beginning of every row until you have 44 sts. Continue to knit until piece measures 5.5 inches from beginning point. Place a marker at the center of the 44sts.

Working on the 22 sts. to the right of the marker, knit 14 "short rows" as follows: adding 2 sts. each row.

Row 1: K2, wrpt (wrap & turn), K2
Row 2: K4, wrpt, K4
Row 3: K6, wrpt, K6
Row 4: K8, wrpt, K8
Row 5: K10, wrpt, K10
Row 6: K12, wrpt, K12
Rows 7-14: Continue with short rows,

adding 2 sts. every row until you have 22 sts. Continue knitting across the second 22 sts. to the end of the row.
Repeat short rows 1 - 14 on the other half of the bottom right piece.
You will now begin to add C2 (2nd color) to fill the V-shaped area you have created with the short rows. Divide remainder of ball of C1 from this section into two balls. Work either side of center from separate balls. (Right side) with Color C1, K21, with color C2, K2, with 2nd ball of color C1, K21.
Continue with two colors of yarn, increasing C2 center stitches by 2 sts. each row & decreasing each side by 1 st. each row as follows:
(WS) K20, K4, K20
K19, K6, K19
K18, K8, K18
K17, K10, K17
K16, K12, K16
K15, K14, K15
K14, K16, K14
K12, K18, K12
K10, K20, K10

Woolscapes

Continue in this manner until all 44 sts are the same color (C2). Cut both balls of C1 yarn and use just C2 at this point. Knit 2 more rows with second color (C2).

Begin 1st striped section: Starting on the RS (right side) with C1, alternate colors every 2 rows to create stripes until the striped section measures 4.5 inches ending on a WS (wrong side) row. Carry yarn along edge when changing colors.

Section with square insert: If previous striped section ended with C1, knit 2 more rows with C2. In this section you will be inserting a square in a contrasting color by "stranding", carrying 2nd color loosely at the back (wrong side) of your work.

Start on the RS with C2, K12. Then, while carrying the yarn at the back of your work, using C1, K10, then, using C2, K22. Continue with square insert as follows, switching yarn color for the square and purling on the wrong side of the insert section.
(WS) K22, P10, K12
(RS) K12, K10, K22
K22, P10, K12

K12, K10, K22
K22, P10, K12
Continue this pattern to complete the square for another 6 rows. Remember, when you are on the wrong side of your work, purl the stitches for the square. (Right Side) With C2, knit 6 rows after completing square. Entire piece should measure approximately 15.5-16 inches from tip of beginning point.

Triangle & Striped Section:
(RS) Row 1 - with color C5, K18, (C3)K26
Row 2 – (C3) K26, (C5) K18 Row 3 – (C2)K18, (C3)K26
Row 4 – (C3)K26, (C2)K18 Row 5 – (C5)K20, (C3)K24
Row 6 – (C3)K24, (C5)K20 Row 7 – (C2)K20 (C3)K24
Row 8 – (C3)K24 (C2)K20 Row 9 – (C5)K22, (C3)K22
Row 10 – (C3)K22, (C5)K22 Row 11 – (C2)K22, (C3)K22
Row 12 – (C3)K22, (C2)K22 Row 13 – (C5)K24, (C3)K20
Row 14 – (C3)K20, (C5)K24 Row 15 – (C2)24, (C3)K20
Row 16 – (C3)K20, (C2)K24 Row 17 – (C5)K18, (C3)K26
Continue this pattern to form triangle, always knitting 2 rows of each color to make stripes, knitting 4 rows of triangle color decreasing triangle edge by 2 sts every 4th row until triangle is complete (total of 36 rows).

Striped Sections: Next 9-10 inches are all knit in garter stitch in a combination of different stripe widths and colors. Suggestion: C5- 3 inches, then alternate in stripes of C5 and C4 for 3", then C4 for 2", then alternate C4 and C3 for 1 inch (total section is 9-10 inches), ending with a wrong side (WS) row.

Square Insert Section: This section will have 2 small inserted squares similar to the larger one that was completed in a section on the lower right front. Starting on the RS of your work, knit 4 rows of garter stitch with C3, ending on a wrong side row. Continue as follows remembering to purl on the wrong side of the square insert sections.

Next row, (RS) with (C3) K23, (C4) K5 (carrying other color on back of work), (C3)K16
WS(C3)K16, (C4)P5, (C3)K23
(C3)K23, (C4)K5, (C3)K16
(C3)K16, (C4)P5, (C3)K23
(C3)K23, (C4)K5, (C3)K6, (C4)K5, (C3)K5
(C3)K5, (C4)P5, (C3)K6, (C4) P5, (C3)K23
(C3)K34, (C4) K5, (C3)K5
(C3) K5, (C4) P5, (C3)K34
(C3)K34, (C4)K5, (C3)K5
(C3)K5, (C4)P5, (C3) K34
(C3) K44, same color across entire row, then knit 7 more rows of garter stitch ending on the wrong side.

Entire piece of work, from beginning point on bottom R- front, should be approximately 37 inches long.

Next Section: Knit 3 inches of garter stitch with (C5), then another 3 inches of garter stitch stripes, using (C5) and (C2) alternating colors every 4 rows. Using the 2nd reserved ball of C1, knit 5 inches of garter stitch adding in a few narrow stripes of a second color if desired.

After completing 5 inches, begin decreases to form point on the bottom of the front left side. Decrease (K2 TOG) at the beginning of every row until 5 stitches remain. Bind off remaining 5 stitches.

This design wraps over the shoulders to form a different kind of arm opening.

This, the first of two pieces to form the shrug, should be 11-12 inches wide X 55 inches long (point to point).

Back panel:
Fold the 1st shrug section in half and mark the center. Place markers 8.5 inches before and after this center mark, defining the center 17". With right side facing you, beginning at first marker, pick up and knit 36 stitches before and after center mark, ending at 3rd marker for a total of 72 stitches across 17 inches. Continue knitting, using desired combination of colors and stripes, for a total of 9.5 inches.

(RS) Switch color to the last reserve ball of C1 for the final section of the lower back.
Knit 1" with C1 ending on a wrong side row, then continue as follows to add inserted rectangle:
(C1)K12, (contrast color)K10, (C1)K22
(C1)K22, (CC)P10, (C1)K12
(C1)K12, (CC)K10, (C1)K22
(C1)K22, (CC)P10, (C1)K12

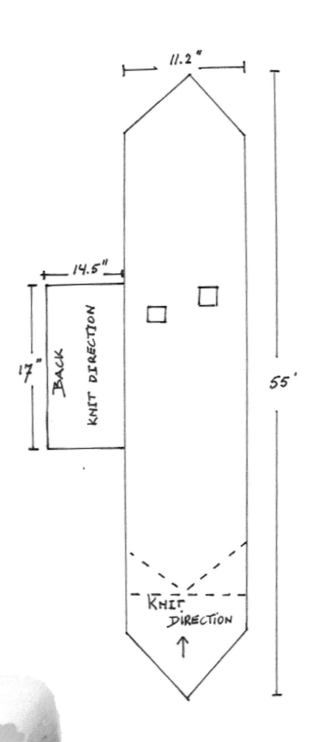

Continue this pattern until you have completed 8 rows of the insert, ending on a wrong side row.

Knit all rows with C1 until this section of C1 measures 5 inches. Bind off all stitches loosely.

Finishing:

Weave in all loose ends on wrong side of shrug. (Tip: When weaving in loose ends, be aware of appearance of wrong side of shrug in the area of the collar that rolls over to expose the wrong side.)

Block entire shrug to desired measurements. Sew bottom 5 inches of fronts and back together on both sides. Determine preferred button placement and add a crochet button loop on the front right edge and a button on the left side.

Child's version:

By using a DK weight yarn and smaller needles (#4 suggested), you can make a smaller version of this vest with just a few adjustments.

Total length of the first piece is 40"

For lower back piece, pick up and knit 62 stitches in the center of the first piece. Knit for 9.5".

Sew the bottom 4" of the fronts and backs together.

Other than these adjustments, follow the directions for the adult vest.

Woolscapes

Bolinas Beanie

This is a different take on the age old and favorite warm beanie. It can be worn many ways and fits most head sizes.

Skill level:
Intermediate

Finished size:
8.5" from top to bottom

Yarn:
1 skein Bo-Rage hand-spun 2 ply, thin worsted, alpaca and wool. Approx. 2oz., 100 yards

Needles:
24" Circular needle size #4 or needle size to obtain gauge. #4 DP needles

Notions:
Embroidery needle
Stitch markers

Gauge:
5 st = 1 inch
6 rows = 1 inch

Stitch pattern:
Half of the hat is in stockinette stitch and half in rib pattern.

General note:
This hat is knit in the round with circular needles until you reach 4.5 inches, with markers at one half of the circle and at full circle. Work one half of the circle in stockinette st. and one half continue in rib pattern. After you reach 4.5", you start decreasing on both sides of the stockinette part of the hat. When all stockinette stitches are decreased, you bind off 1/3 of the rib stitches (approx. 16 st. each side) on both sides of the stockinette side and reduce the remaining stitches to a point that will be sewn together to create the distinctive top of the hat.

Hat:
Cast on 92 st.
Knit in rib pattern (K2, P2) for 2 inches, approx. 14 rows.
Place a green marker at stitch 1 and a red marker at stitch 46.
Knit the first 46 st. then K and P the remaining st. in rib pattern, so half the hat will be in stockinette pattern and the other half in K2, P2 rib pattern. Work in this pattern for 2.5 inches until you have 4.5 inches total.
Decreases start in the stockinette section as follows:
At the green stitch marker, K2 TOG, knit 44 st. and at the red stitch marker SSK. (Make sure these decreases fall within the stockinette part of the hat). Continue with K2 and P2 rib pattern to the end of the row.
Repeat this row until you have 3 stitches left on the stockinette side of the hat, approx. 7".
K2 TOG, pull last stitch over the remaining st. (1 stitch left). Put this stitch onto the left needle and K2 TOG. You now have 46 rib stitches.
Divide the 46 st. in 3 parts on DP needles: 16 st. on needle 1, 14 st. on needle 2 (middle needle) and 16 st. on needle 3.

Bind off all the stitches on needle 1, work the stitches on needle 2 and 3.
Turn, bind off the stitches on needle 3. You now have 14 stitches left (on needle 2).
Bind off 2 stitches at the beginning and rib to the end.
Bind off 2 stitches at the beginning and rib to the end.
Repeat until there are no stitches left.
Fold the point over and bring it to the point of the stockinette side. Sew along the bind off edges into a triangle. Sew on the wrong side of the hat.

Finishing;
Weave in all loose ends.

Four Panel Vest

This vest consists of four panels that are almost identical, except for the front neck edge. Each panel is started at the corner with 3 stitches, then increased on each side of the middle diagonal line, until you have 67 stitches. Next you bind off about half the stitches and continue with the upper body. All panels are sewn together, after which the neck and armhole edges are finished. All panels have a 4 stitch edging (garter st). When sewn together, these edges form a decorative element for the back seam and front band.

Skill level:
Intermediate

Measurements:
This vest fits a medium size person. Only one size is given.

Finished size:
Bust circumference 32"
Length from shoulder to bottom edge 24"

Yarn:
Bo-Rage mill-spun, heavy worsted, 2 ply, approx. 700 yards
Commercial available equivalent is Brown Sheep, Lamb's Pride worsted weight

Needles:
Size # 8 (5mm) or needle size to obtain gauge.

Gauge:
4 stitches = 1 inch
6 rows = 1 inch

Notions:
Tapestry needle
Stitch markers
Stitch holder or spare circular needle

Right front panel
Cast on 3 st.
Row 1: Knit
Row 2: K1, YO, K1,YO,K1 (5 st)
Row 3: K2, P1, K2
Continue in this manner until you have 67 st.
Row 64: K32, YO, K1, YO, K32 (67 st)
You now have completed a rectangle with two sides of 11" and 2 sides of 9".
Next, on the WS, bind off 34 st. There will be 33 st remaining.
Continue in St. St. until piece measures 20", maintaining the garter st. edge as follows:

Woolscapes

Row 1: Starting on the WS, P29, K4

Row 2: RS, K 33

Repeat these two rows until piece measures 20".

Next, on the RS, bind off 14 st. There will be 19 stitches remaining.

Continue in St.St. for 4 inches.

Bind off in pattern.

Left front panel

Follow instructions for right front panel until you have completed the rectangle.

Next, on the WS, bind off 34 sts. There will be 33 sts remaining.

Continue in St.St. until pieces measures 20" while maintaining the front garter st. edge as follows:

Row 1: Starting on the RS, K33.

Row 2: K4, P29. Repeat until piece measures 20".

Next, on the WS, bind off 14 st. There will be 19 st. remaining.

Continue in St.St. for 4".

Bind off.

Right back panel:

Follow instructions for right front until you have completed the rectangle.

Next, on the RS, bind off 34 st. There will be 33 sts. remaining.

Continue in St.St until piece measured 24", following the same instructions as for the left front panel to maintain the back garter stitch edge.

Bind off.

Left back panel:

Follow instructions for right front panel until you have completed the rectangle.

Next, on the WS, bind off 34 st. There will be 33 sts. remaining.

Continue in St. St. until piece measures 24", following the same instructions as for the right front panel to maintain the back garter st. edge.

Bind off.

Sew shoulder seams together. With wrong sides facing sew 19 stitches from front panel to 19 stitches from back panel. Put the remaining 28 stitches for back of neck on a holder (a spare circular needle works well).

Neck band:

With right side facing, PU 90 stitches as follows: Knit across 24 st from left front horizontal edge, PM, 17 stitches from left front vertical edge. K 28 stitches from back of neck edge, K 17 stitches from right side vertical edge, PM, and K 14 stitches from right side front horizontal. Work in rib (P2, K2) for 1.5 inches.

At the same time decrease one stitch every row at each of the two mitered corners for 5 rows.

Miter method:

Note: You will have to reposition marker after each decrease.

Note: When decreasing at the mitered corners you will have to adjust for the change in stitch count in order to maintain the rib pattern for rest of neck edge.

Row 1: with wrong side facing, P2, K2 for 13 stitches, P2 TOG using the two stitches on either side of marker, continue in rib pattern until there are 15 st. left on needle, P2 TOG using the two stitches on either side of the marker, continue in K2, P2 rib pattern for rest of row. You should end the row with P2.

Row 2: With right side facing, K2, P2 for 12 stitches,

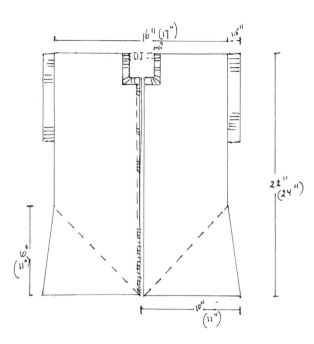

Armhole:

Sew side seams, leaving a 10 ½ " opening for armhole. Pick up 84 stitches (if another size is desired, PU a multiple of 4, i.e. 80 or 88). Knit in a rib pattern starting with P2, K2 (wrong side facing) for 1 ½ inches.
Bind off in rib pattern.

Finishing:

Weave in all ends.
Block lightly with a steam iron.

K2 TOG (again using the two stitches on either side of marker), continue in pattern until there are 14 stitches left, K2 TOG, continue in rib ending with K2.

Continue in this manner for three more rows.
Bind off in rib pattern.

West Marin Cap

In Holland the farmers used to wear caps with visors in the field. Sundays in church when they had to take off their hats, you could see the white ring where the sun never reached and their frayed, frost- bitten ears. I always wondered why they did not make the hat band wider so they could pull it over their ears. So here is that imagined hat.

Skill level:
Easy to intermediate

Finished size:
7.5" from top to bottom rim
9" diameter

Yarn:
One skein of Bo-Rage mill-spun dark tweed, or a 2 ply thin worsted weight yarn. Approx. 4 oz., 200 yards Equivalent commercial yarn is Cascade 220 worsted weight

Needles:
24" circular #7 needle or needle size to obtain gauge. Main needle Double pointed #7 needles 24" circular #6 needles for the band and visor

Notions:
Stitch markers

Tapestry needle
Measuring tape

Gauge:
4 st = 1inch
6 rows = 1inch

General note:
The hat band of this cap is deeper (wider) in the back than in the front. This is done by means of short rows. The short rows are made easier if you use two different colored markers. You divide the stitches of the row in half. Use the green marker as the beginning of your row and the red marker at the halfway mark. After the cap is finished, the visor is knit onto it. The visor is doubled to make it stand out a bit.

Band of the cap:
For the band pattern: rib in K2, P2.
Cast on 100 st. with needle size #6.
At the beginning stitch, put your green stitch marker and at 50 st. put your red marker. Join the stitches to form a circle.
Knit in rib pattern (K2, P2) for 3 rows.
Row 4: (this is a short row) work in K2, P2 to the red

Structural Elements

marker, W&T (wrap and turn) and work in pattern, back
to the green marker.

Row 5: Work the whole row in pattern back to the
green marker.

Repeat rows 4 and 5, four times until
the band measures 1.5" in the front
and 3" in the back.

Body of the cap:

Next knit all stitches for 8 full rows.

Next row: *M1, K10* (increase 1st
stitch every 10 stitches). Repeat to
end of row (110 st.).

Next row: M1, K11, repeat to end of row, (120
st.).

Next row: M1, K12 , repeat to end of row, (130 st.).

Next row: M1, K 13, repeat to end of row, (140 st.).

The increase always falls on the same stitch and forms
a decorative line.

Next, knit 3 rows without increases.

Crown of the cap:

Now the decreases start at the same points where you
increased.

Next row: K2 TOG, K14 (decrease 1 stitch every 14
stitches), repeat to end of row.

Next row: K2 TOG, K13, repeat to end of row.

Next row: K2 TOG, K12, repeat to end of row.

Next row: K2 TOG, K11, repeat to end of row.

Next row: K2 TOG, K10, repeat to end of row.

Next row: K2 TOG, K9, repeat to end of row.

Next row: K2 TOG, K8, repeat to end of row.

Next row: K2 TOG, K7, repeat to end of row.

Next row: K2 TOG, K6, repeat to end of row.

By now you probably will want to change to DP needles to work more easily on fewer stitches.

Next row: Knit whole row without decreases.

Next row: K2 TOG, K5

Next row: Knit whole row without decreases.

Next row: K2 TOG, K4

Next row: Knit whole row without decreases.

Next row: K2 TOG, K3

Continue in the manner until you have 6 stitches left. Break the yarn. Thread a tapestry needle and pull the thread through these stitches and weave the loose end into the wrong side of the cap.

Visor:
Pick up 30 st. on the front (short) side of the cap 6 st. away from each marker.
Row 1: K (with the RS facing you)
Row 2: P
Next row: K2 TOG, K to last 2 stitches, K2 TOG.
Next row: P2 TOG, P to last 2 stitches, P2 TOG.
Repeat these 2 rows one more time. (22 st. left)
Next row: Bind off 5 st. at the beginning of the knit row. K to end of row.
Next row: Bind off 5 st. at the beginning of the purl row. P to end of row (12 st. left).
Next row: K

Next row: K (this gives the cap the ridge at the point of the visor)
This is where the visor is turned. You are now starting the mirror image of the visor.
Next row: Cast on 5 st., K to end of row.
Next row: Cast on 5 st., P to end of row.
Next row: M1 st. and K to the last stitch, M1.
Next row: M1 st. and P to the last stitch, M1.
Repeat these 2 rows one more time.
Next row: K
Next row: P
Bind off.
Sew the visor together on the wrong side and turn right side out and sew the bottom side of the visor to the cap's band.

Finishing:
Weave in all loose ends and lightly block the cap.

Plowline Cardigan

The lines in the dark earth after a field is plowed were the inspiration for this sweater. When I grew up in Holland, the farmers plowed the land with draft horses. Now here in Bolinas there are small hidden plots of land, in-between the trees and shrubs where young farmers grow their organic crops in similar linear mounds.

Skill Level:
Experienced

Finished Size:
Total Length: 22.5" from neck opening to bottom
Length to armhole: 12"
Armhole length: 6.5"
Right and left front width: 11"
Back width: 19"

Yarn:
Bo-Rage Mill Spun Single, Lopi. Heavy worsted weight or possibly a light chunky.
Commercial yarn equivalent is Lamb's Pride burly spun.
Amount of yarn needed is 1400 yards/ seven skeins, 200 yards each (4oz).

Needles:
8 MN (main needle) and #6 SN(smaller needle) or sizes needed to obtain gauge.

Gauge:
3.5 stitches = 1 inch
4.5 rows = 1 inch.

Notions:
Cable needle
Wool needle or tapestry needle
Stitch marker

Stitch Patterns
Rib pattern
Traveling stitch patterns

General Note:
This sweater is knit from the top down. The front button band is picked up after the sweater body is complete. The band stitches are picked up and knit horizontally in the rib pattern.

Back:
CO 50 stitches with MN. PM at the halfway point (25sts). Start the rib pattern, making sure the two middle sts are purls. To do this start with P2, K2, ending with P2. Knit the rib pattern for 10 rows.
Row 11: R20, C4PB, P2, C4KF, R20.
Row 12: and all even numbered rows: K & P in pattern.
Row 13: R18, C4B, P6, C4F, R18.
Row 15: R16, C4PB, K2, P6, K2, C4KF, R16.
Row 17: R14, C4B, P2, K2, P6, K2, P2, C4F, R14
Row 19: R12, C4PB, K2, P2, K2, P6, K2, P2, K2, C4KF, R12.
Row 20: CO 14sts using the knitted CO method, CIP, (64sts).
Row 21: CO 14sts using the knitted CO method, R24, CB4, R8, P6, R8, C4F, R24 (78sts).
Row 23: R22, C4PB, rib10, P6, R10, C4KF, R22.
Row 25: R20, C4B, R12, P6, R12, C4F, R20.
Row 27: R18, C4PB, R14, P6, R10, C4KF, R18.
Row 29: R16, C4B, R14, P6, R14, C4F, R16.
Start of center pattern.

Row 31: R14, C4PB, R16, K3, P4, K3, R16, C4KF, R14.
Row 33: R12, C4B, R18, K4, P2, K4, R18, C4K, R12.
Row 35: R10, C4PB, R20, K10, R20, C4KF, R10.
Row 37: R8, C4B, R22, TSL, K6, TSR, R22, C4F, R8.
Row 39: R6, C4PB, R24, K1, TSL, K4, TSR, K1, R24, C4KF, R6.
Row 41: R4, C4B, R26, K2, TSL, K2, TSR, K2, R26, C4F, R4.
Row 43: R2, C4PB, R28, K3, TSL, TSR, K3, R28, C4KF, R2.

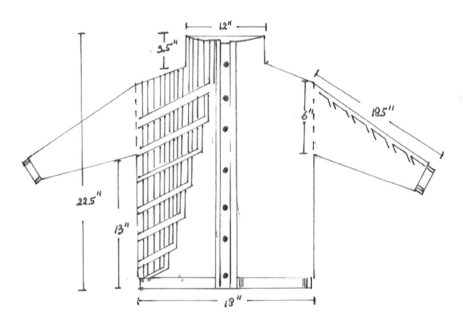

Row 45: C4B, R30, K4, S2, K4, R30, C4F.

Row 47: K4, R30, P2, K4, S2, K4, R30, K4.

Row 49: K4, R28, P1, K5, S2, K5, P1, R28, K4.

Row 51: K4, R26, TSL, K6, S2, K6, TSR, R26, K4.

Row 53: K4, R26, K1, TSL, K5, SL2, K5, TSR, K1, R26, K4.

Row 55: K4, R26, K2, TSL, K4, SL2, K4, TSR, K2, R26, K4

Row 57: K4, R26, K3, TSL, K3, SL2, K3, TSR, K3, R26, K4.

Row 59: K4, R26, K4, TSL, K2, SL2, K2, TSR, K4, R26, K4.

Row 61: K4, R26, K5, TSL, K1, SL2, K1, TSR, K5, R26, K4.

Row 63: K4, R26, K6, TSL, SL2, TSR, K6, R26, K4.

Row 65: K4, R26, K7, TSL, TSR, K7, R26, K4.

Row 67: K4, R26, K8, SL2, K8, R26, K4.

Row 69: K4, R22, TSL, P2, K8, S2, K8, P2, TSR, R22, K4.

Row 71: K4, R22, K1, TSL, K9, S2, K9, TSR, K1, R22, K4.

Row 73: K4, R22, K2, TSL, K8, S2, K8, TSR, K2, R22, K4.

Row 75: K4, R22, K3, TSL, K7, S2, K7, TSR, K3, R22, K4.

Row 77: K4, R22, K4, TSL, K6, S2, K6, TSR, K4, R22. K4.

Row 79: K4, R22, K5, TSL, K5, S2, K5, TSR, K5, R22, K4.

Row 81: K4, R22, K6, TSL, K4, S2, K4, TSR, K6, R22, K4.

Row 83: K4, R22, K7, TSL, K3, S2, K3, TSR, K7, R22, K4.

Row 85: K4, R22, K8, TSL, K2, S2, K2, TSR, K8, R22, K4.

Row 87: K4, R22, K9, TSL, K1, S2, K1, TSR, K9, R22, K4.

Row 89: K4, R22, K10, TSL, S2, TSR, K10, R22, K4.
Row 91: K4, R22, K11, TSL, TSR, K11, R22, K4.
Row 93: K4, R18, TSL, P1, K13, S2, K13, P1, TSR, R18, K4.
Row 95: K4, R18, K1, TSL, K13, S2, K13, TSR, K1, R18, K4.
Row 97: K4, R18, K2, TSL, K12, S2, K12, TSR, K2, R18, K4.
Row 99: K4, R18, K3, TSL, K11, S2, K11, TSR, K3, R18, K4.
Row 101: K4, R18, K4, TSL, K10, S2, K10, TSR, K4, R18, K4.
Row 103: K4, R18, K5, TSL, K9, S2, K9, TSR, K5, R18, K4.
Row 105: K4, R18, K6, TSL, K8, S2, K8, TSR, K6, R18, K4.
Row 107: K4, R18, K7, TSL, K7, S2, K7, TSR, K7, R18, K4.
Row 109: K4, R18, K8, TSL, K6, S2, K6, TSR, K8, R18, K4.
Row 111: K4, R18, K9, TSL, K5, S2, K5, TSR, K9, R18, K4.
Row 113: K4, R18, K10, TSL, K4, S2, K4, TSR, K10, R18, K4.
Row 115: K4, R18, K11, TSL, K3, S2, K3, TSR, K11, R18, K4.
Row 117: K4, R18, K12, TSL, K2, S2, K2, TSR, K12, R18, K4.
Row 119: K4, R18, K13, TSL, K1, S2, K1, TSR, K13, R18, K4.
Row 121: K4, R18, K14, TSL, S2, TSR, K14, R18, K4.
Start lower edge ribbing with the rib pattern (K2, P2,) for 10 rows.
BO in pattern.

Right Front:
CO 30sts.
Row 1: *K2, P2*, repeat to last 4sts, P4.
Row 2: And for all even numbered row, K the knits and P the purls.
Repeat rows 1 and 2 three times for a total of 8 rows.
Start of the traveling cables.
Row 9: R22, C4KF, P4.
Row 11: R20, C4B, P6.
Row 13: R18, C4KF, K2, P6.
Row 15: R16, C4B, P2, K2, P6.
Row 17: R14, C4KF, R6, P6.
Row 19: R12, C4B, R8, P6.
Row 21: CO 14sts using the knitted CO method, rib24, C4KF, rib6, C4KF, P6. (44sts)

Row 23: R22, C4B, R6, C4B, P8.
Row 25: R20, C4BF, R6, C4BF, K2, P8.
Row 27: R18, C4B, R6, C4B, R4, P8.
Row 29: R16, C4KB, R6, C4KB, R6, P8.
Row 31: R14, C4B, R6, C4B, R8, P8.
Row 33: R12, C4KB, R6, C4KB, R6, C4KB, P8.
Row 35: R10, C4B, R6, C4B, R6, C4B, P10.
Row 37: R8, C4KB, R6, C4KB, R6, C4KB, K2, P10.
Row 39: R6, C4B, R6, C4B, R6, C4B, R4, P10.
Row 41: R4, C4PB, R6, C4PB, R6, C4PB, R6, P10.
Row 43: K2, C4B, R6, C4B, R6, C4B, R8, P10.
Row 45: C4PB, R6, C4PB, R6, C4PB, R6, C4PB, P10.
Row 47: R8, C4B, R6, C4B, R6, C4B, P12.

Woolscapes

Row 49: R6, C4PB, R6, C4PB, R6, C4PB, K2, P12.
Row 51: K4, C4B, R6, C4B, R6, C4B, R4, P12.
Row 53: K2, C4PB, R6, C4PB, R6, C4PB, R6, P12.
Row 55: C4B, R6, CRB, R6, CRB, R8, P12.
Row 57: K4, R4, C4PB, rib 6, C4PB, R6, C4PB, P12.
Row 59: K4, P2, C4B, R6, C4B, R6, C4B, P14.
Row 61: K4, C4PB, R6, C4PB, R6, C4PB, K2, P14.
Row 63: K2, C4B, R6, C4B, R6, C4B, R4, P14.
Row 65: C4PB, R6, C4PB, R6, C4PB, R6, P14.
Row 67: R8, C4B, R6, C4B, R8, P14.
Row 69: R6, C4PB, R6, C4PB, R6, C4PB, P14.
Row 71: R4, C4B, R6, C4B, R6, C4B, P16.
Row 73: K2, C4PB, R6, C4PB, R6, C4PB, K2, P16.
Row 75: C4B, R6, C4B, R6, C4B, R4, P16.
Row 77: K2, R6, C4PB, R6, C4PB, R6, P16.
Row 79: K2, R4, C4B, R6, C4B, R8, P16.
Row 81: K4, C4PB, R6, C4PB, R6, C4PB, P16.
Row 83: K2, C4B, R6, C4B, R6, C4B, P18.

Row 85: C4PB, R6, C4PB, R6, C4PB, K2, P18.
Row 87: R8, C4B, R6, C4B, R4, P18.
Row 89: R6, C4PB, R6, C4PB, R6, P18.
Row 91: R4, C4B, R6, C4B, R8, P18.
Row 93: K2, C4PB, R6, C4PB, R6, C4PB, P18.
Row 95: C4B, R6, C4B, R6, C4B, P20.
Row 97: K4, R4, C4PB, R6, C4PB, K2, P20.
Row 99: K2, R4, C4B, R6, C4B, R4, P20.
Row 101: K4, C4PB, R6, C4PB, R6, P20.
Row 103: K2, C4B, R6, C4B, R8, P20.
Row 105: C4PB, R6, C4PB, R6, C4PB, P20.
Row 107: R8, C4B, R6, C4B, P22.
Row 109: R6, C4PB, R6, C4PB, K2, P22.
Row 111: R4, C4B, R6, C4B, R4, P22.
Row 113: K2, C4PB, R6, C4PB, R6, P22.
Row 115: C4B, R6, C4B, R8, P22.
Row 117: K2, R6, C4PB, R6, C4PB, P24.
Row 119: K4, P2, C4B, R6, C4B, P24.

Row 121: K2, P2, C4PB, R6, C4PB, K2, P24.
Start rib for the bottom border starting with P2, K2.
Continue in rib pattern for 10 rows.

BO.

Left Front:
The left front is a mirror image of the right front.
CO 30sts.
Row 1: P4, *K2, P2*, repeat ** to end of row.
Row 2: and all even numbered rows: Knit the knits, and
    purl the purls.
Repeat rows 1 and 2 for a total of 8 rows.
Start traveling cables.
Row 9: P4, C4KF, R22.
Row 11: P6, C4F, R20.
Row 13: P6, K2, C4KF, R18.
Row 15: P6, K2, P2, C4F, R16.
Row 17: P6, R6, C4KF, R14.
Row 19: P6, R8, C4F, R12.
Row 20: WS, CO 14sts using the knitted CO method.
    R4, CIP to end of row. (44sts)
Row 21: P6, C4KF, R6, C4KF, R24.
Row 23: P8, C4F, R6, C4F, R22.
Row 25: P8, K2, C4KF, R6, C4KF, R20.
Row 27: P8, R4, C4F, R6, C4F, R18.
Row 29: P8, R6, C4KF, R6, C4KF, R16.
Row 31: P8, R8, C4F, R6, C4F, R14.
Row 33: P8, C4KF, R6, C4KF, R6, C4KF, R12.
Row 35: P10, C4F, R6, C4F, R6, C4F, R10.
Row 37: P10, K2, C4KF, R6, C4KF, R6, C4KF, R8.
Row 39: P10, R4, C4F, R6, C4F, rib6, C4F, R6.
Row 41: P10, R6, C4KF, R6, C4KP, R6, C4KF, R4.
Row 43: P10, R8, C4F, R6, C4F, R6, C4F, K2.
Row 45: P10, C4KF, R6, C4KF, R6, C4KF, R6, C4KF.
Row 47: P12, C4F, R6, C4F, R6, C4F, R8.
Row 49: P12, K2, C4KF, R6, C4KF, R6, C4KF, R6.
Row 51: P12, R4, C4F, R6, C4F, R6, C4F, K4.
Row 53: P12, R6, C4KF, R6, C4KF, R6, C4KF, K2.
Row 55: P12, R8, C4F, R6, C4F, R6, C4F.
Row 57: P12, C4KF, R6, C4KF, R6, C4KF, R4, K4.
Row 59: P14, C4F, R6, C4F, R6, C4F, P2, K4.

Woolscapes

Row 61: P14, K2, C4KF, R6, C4KF, R6, C4KF, K4.
Row 63: P14, R4, C4F, R6, C4F, R6, C4F, K2.
Row 65: P14, R6, C4KF, R6, C4KF, R6, C4KF.
Row 67: P14, R8, C4F, R6, C4F, R8.
Row 69: P14, C4KF, R6, C4KF, R6, C4KF, R6.
Row 71: P16, C4F, R6, C4F, R6, C4F, R4.
Row 73: P16, K2, C4KF, R6, C4KF, R6, C4KF, K2.
Row 75: P16, R4, C4F, R6, C4F, R6, C4F.
Row 77: P16, R6, C4KF, R6, C4KF, R6, K2.
Row 79: P16, R8, C4F, R6, C4F, R4, K2.
Row 81: P16, C4KF, R6, C4KF, R6, C4KF, R4.
Row 83: P18, C4F, R6, C4F, R6, C4F, K2.
Row 85: P18, K2, C4KF, R6, C4KF, R6, C4KF.
Row 87: P18, R4, C4F, R6, C4F, R8.
Row 89: P18, R6, C4KF, R6, C4KF, R6.
Row 91: P18, R8, C4F, R6, C4F, R4.
Row 93: P18, C4KF, R6, C4KF, R6, C4KF, K2.
Row 95: P20, C4F, R6, C4F, R6, C4F.
Row 97: P20, K2, C4KF, R6, C4KF, R4, K4.
Row 99: P20, R4, C4F, R6, C4F, R4, K2.
Row 101: P20, R6, C4KF, R6, C4KF, K4.
Row 103: P20, R8, C4F, R6, C4F, K2.
Row 105: P20, C4KF, R6, C4KF, R6, C4F.
Row 107: P22, C4F, R6, C4F, R8.
Row 109: P22, K2, C4KF, R6, C4KF, R6.
Row 111: P22, R4, C4F, R6, C4F, R4.
Row 113: P22, R6, C4KF, R6, C4KF, K2.
Row 115: P22, R8, C4F, R6, C4F.
Row 117: P24, C4KF, R6, C4KF, R6, K2.
Row 119: P24, C4F, R6, C4F, P2, K4.
Row 121: P24, K2, C4KF, R6, C4KF, P2, K2.
Start rib (K2, P2) for bottom border. CIP for 10 rows.
BO
Sew together shoulders and collar.

Sleeves:
Pick up 58sts, 29sts from front and 29sts from back.
Stockinette stitch for 10 rows.
Start of the Travel Stitch Pattern.
Row 11: K26, P2, K2, P2, K26.
Row 12: And all even numbered rows, K & P in pattern.

or when the 5th TS pattern is complete.
Change to smaller size needles and knit the ribbed cuff (K2, P2) for 2-2 ½".
BO in pattern.

Travel Stitch Pattern (TSP) for sleeves:

The TSP the sleeves is 10 stitches in width and 16 rows in length.
Row 1: K2, P2, K2, P2, K2.
Row 3-8: Repeat rows 1 & 2.
Row 9: K2, P1, TSRP, TSLP, P1, K2.
Row 11: K2, TSRP, P2, TSLP, K2.
Row 13: K1, TSRP, P4, TSLP, K1.
Row 15: TSR, P6, TSL.
Row 16: K + P in pattern.

Front Bands:
Left Front Band:

PU 86sts on RS, 3sts in from front edge. This will cause the front band to have a rolled back lip before starting the ribbing, a nice feature.
On RS, start the front band ribbing (K2, P2,) ending
   with K2.
Continue ribbing for, 1 ½".
BO in pattern.

Right Front Band:

Follow instructions for left front band, but add 8 buttonholes, evenly spaced.

Finishing:

Sew on buttons and weave in loose ends.
Gently block sweater with a steam iron. Avoid putting the iron directly on the sweater.

Rows 13 – 18: Repeat rows 11 & 12.
Row 19: K26, P1, TSRP, TSLP, P1, K26.
Row: 21: K26, TSRP, P2, TSLP, K26.
Row 23: K25, TSRP, P4, TSLP, K25.
Row 25: K24, TSR, P6, TSL, K24.
When sleeve measures 6", start decreases. On the RS, dec. one stitch at beg. & end of every 6th row. When sleeve measures 9", dec. every 4 rows. At the same time continue in the traveling stitch pattern which runs down center of sleeve until 32-28 stitches remain

PART TWO

NATURAL COLORED GARMENTS

Surface Elements

In this section of Natural Colored Garments, we will look at surface design and surface elements.

These local wools are ideal for textural surface design because they have perfect stitch definition. This shows up very well in the lighter shades of the natural colors.

To achieve this different textural look for these rustic, natural colored yarns, we used cables, traveling stitches and lace stitches as well as different shades of natural colors.

The structural elements of these garments are more straightforward than in the previous section. The difference lies within the treatment of the "fabric" of the garment.

With hand-knitting you can manipulate the yarn in such a way as to create a "fabric" that is unique. Cables can give you a scalloped edge, while a traveling stitch can guide your eye towards a different section of the garment. Different colors can highlight certain points in a vest, and with a lace stitch you can lighten the appearance as well as the physical weight of a garment.

Briones Vest

Briones are a historic family in Bolinas. They settled the lands around Dogtown and Las Baulinas, as it was called in these days. This vest was created because in my knit basket were all these natural colored skeins. They looked so enticing together, I decided to create something with these muted rustic colors that reflect the lands around Dogtown and Bolinas. The vest is reminiscent of vests men wore around the time of Dogtown's settlement.

Skill level:
Easy, ideal for a first intarsia project

Measurements:
This sample is for a medium size person. It can easily be made larger by adding several stitches on the front panel sides and back panel sides and lengthening the vest.

Finished size: (size given is medium)
Total length: 21" (this includes the 3" of the front points)
Back Length: 18"
Length to armhole: 9"
Armhole length: 9"
Front width: 10.5"

Yarn:
Bo-Rage mill-spun, 2 ply, worsted, two natural colors, total 800 yards
Commercial available yarn equivalent is Brown Sheep Lamb's Pride worsted weight

Needles:
Size #8, or needle size to obtain gauge. Main needle
Size #6 for arm opening border bands

Notions:
Embroidery needle
Stitch markers
Stitch holders
Measuring tape

Gauge:
3.5 st = 1 inch
5 rows = 1 inch

Stitch pattern:
Stockinette for the body of the vest
Seed stitch for the borders

General note:
This vest is a perfect first intarsia project. The rectangles are simple and only two colors are used at the same time. In the back for the large rectangle, three balls of yarn are used, (only two colors, but in three different places). For the smaller squares and stripes, the main color is stranded in order to keep the number of yarn balls to a minimum.

This vest is knit from the bottom to the top. The arm opening border bands are not knit at the same time in order to minimize the "intarsia" yarn balls used. After

Surface Elements

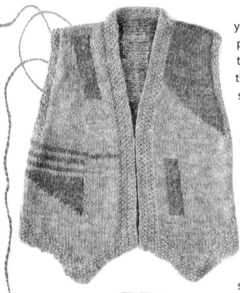

you finish the vest, you pick up stitches around the arm opening and knit the border band in seed stitch.

For the fronts, you start with the point and add stitches. The front border is knit in seed stitch at the same time. It is imperative that you work with a measuring tape to decide when to decrease for the arms and when to start a new color.

Back:
Cast on 60 st. with color 1 (C1)

K and P in seed st (+). for 2", approx. 12 rows

Row 13: start stockinette stitch (++) and work for 3" (approx. 16 rows) until you reach 5" from the bottom.

Next start with color 2 (C2) for the rectangle insert. Use a second ball of C1 for the other side of the rectangle, so you are working with three balls of yarn (of which two balls are the same color).

With RS facing you, K 15st. (C1), K 30 st. (C2), K15 st. (C1).

Purl back in color scheme. Make sure to wrap your yarn where the color changes

Repeat these 2 rows for 4" more until you reach 9" from the bottom.

Here decrease for the arm opening

With RS facing you, bind off 6 st: K9 (C1), K30 (C2), K15 (C1).

With WS facing you, bind off 6 st., P9 (C1), P30 (C2), P9 (C1).

Continue in established pattern until you reach 12" from the bottom.

Next introduce C1 square in the C2 rectangle. This is where the middle section is stranded (woven in the back). You carry C2 over to the other side of the middle C1 section.

Next row: *K9 (C1), K10 (C2), K10 (C1), (while stranding C2) K10 (C2), K9 (C1)

Purl back in color pattern stranding in the same part)*

Repeat these 2 rows for 2.5".

Next row: **RS facing you, K9 with C1, K30 with C2, K9 with C1.

Next row, purl in color pattern**.

Repeat * for 4 more rows.

Repeat ** for 2 more rows.

Repeat * for 2 more rows.

Repeat ** for 2 more rows.

Continue until you have 19.5".

Bind off

Right front:
Work the first part in seed st. You will increase 2 stitches every row and then work the next row without increases. So you M1 st. at the beginning and M1 st. at the end of every second row until you reach 2".

Cast on 5 st. with C1.

Row 1: K1, P1 (seed st.) to end of row (5 st.).

Row 2: M1, K1, P1 (seed st.) to end of row and M1. (7 st.)

Row 3: (and all uneven rows) work in seed st.

Row 4: M1, work in seed st. to end of row, M1 (9 st.)

Repeat to row 12. You will have 15 st. Mark the middle st. (PM)

Row 12: M1, Seed st. to middle st. K middle st. Knit the next 3 st. (you are breaking the seed st. pattern and starting the stockinette pattern) and work in seed st. to the end of row.

Row 13: Cast on 5 st., 12 st., seed pattern, P3, work in seed st. to end of row. (21 st.)

Row 14: Cast on 5 st., 11 st., seed pattern, K5, work in seed st. to the end of row. (26 st.)

Row 15: Cast on 5 st., 15 st., seed pattern, P5, work in seed st. to the of row. (31 st.)

Row 16: Cast on 5 st.,15 st., seed pattern, K7, work in seed st. to the end of row. (36 st.)

Row 17: Cast on 4 st., 18 st., seed pattern, P9, work in seed st. to end of row. (40 st.)

Row 18: Seed 12 st., K11 st., seed to end of row.

Row 19: Seed 17 st., P11 st., seed to end of row.

Row 20: Seed 12 st., K12 st., seed to end of row.

Row 21: Seed 15 st., P15 st., seed to end of row.

Row 22: Seed 9 st., K17 st., seed to end of row.

Row 23: Seed 13 st., P19 st., seed to end of row.

Row 24: Seed 11 st., K23 st., seed 6 (this is the start of your border band).

Row 25: Seed 11 st., P23 st., seed to end of row.

Row 26: Seed 6 st., K27 st., seed to end of row.

Row 27: Seed 6 st., P to last 6 st., seed 6 st.

Row 28: Seed 6 st., K29 st., seed to end of row.

Row 29: Seed 3 st., P31, seed 6 st.

Row 30: Seed 6 st., K34 to end of row.

Row 31: P34, seed 6 st.

Repeat these last 2 rows one more time.

Next introduce a new color: C2

Row 34: Seed 6 st., K11, K1 (C2), K to end of row (C1).

Row 35: P21, P2 (C2), P11, Seed 6 st.

Row 36: Seed 6 st., K11, K3 (C2), K(C1) to end of row (at this point, strand C1 behind C2).

Row 37: P19, P4 (C2) , P11, Seed 6 st.

Row 38: Seed 6 st., K11, K5 (C2) K (C1) to end of row.

Row 39: P17, P6 (C2) P11, Seed 6 st.

Row 40: Seed 6 st., K11, K7 (C2) K to end.

Row 41: P15, P8 (C2) P11, Seed 6 st.

Row 42: Seed 6 st., K11, K9(C2) K to end.

Row 43: P13, P10 (C2) ,P11, Seed 6 st.

Row 44: Seed 6 st., K11, K 11 (C2), K to end.

Row 45: P11, P 12 (C2) , P11,Seed 6 st.

Row 46: Seed 6 st., K11, K13(C2) K to end.

Row 47: P9, P12 (C2) P11, Seed 6 st.

Row 48: Seed 6 st., K11, K13 (C3) K to end.

Row 49: P7, P16 (C2)m P11, Seed 6 st.

Row 50: Seed 6 st., K11, K17 (C2), K to end.

Row 51: P5, P 18 (C2), P11, Seed 6 st.

Row 52: Seed 6 st., K22, K19 (C2) K to end.

Row 53: P3, P20 (C2) P11, Seed 6 st.

Row 54: Seed 6 st., K11, K21 with C2 to end of row.

Row 55: P1, P22 (C2) P11, Seed 6 st.

Row 56: Seed 6 st., K 34 with C1.

Row 57: P 34, Seed 6 st.

Row 58: Seed 6 st., K11, K23 with C2 .

Row 59: Purl 23 (C2) P11, Seed 6 st.

Row 60: Seed 6 st., K34

Row 61: P34, seed 6 st.

Row 62: Seed 6 st., K11, K23 with C2.

Row 63: P23 (C2) P11, Seed 6 st.

Row 64: Seed 6 st., K34.

Row 65: P34, Seed 6 st.

Row 66: Seed 6 st., K11, K23 with C2.

Row 67: P23, (C2) continue P11 (C2) but strand C1, seed 6 st. (C1)

Row 68: Seed 6 st., K11(C2) stranded, K 23 (you should have approx. 12" from the bottom point, 9.5" from the seam side).

Next decrease for the armhole.

Row 69: Bind off 7 st. P to last 6 and seed 6 st.

Decrease for the V-Neck. These are done in the center of the front panel and decreases are done every 6 rows. Here is also the one short row for the border band to allow for the bend in the garment.

Row 70 (a): Seed 6 st., turn, seed 6 st. back.

Row 70 (b): Seed 6, K8, K2 TOG, K to end of row (32 st.).

Row 71: P to last 6 st., seed 6 st.

Row 72: Seed 6 st., K to end of row.

Row 73: P26, seed 6 st.

Row 74: Seed 6 st., K to end of row.

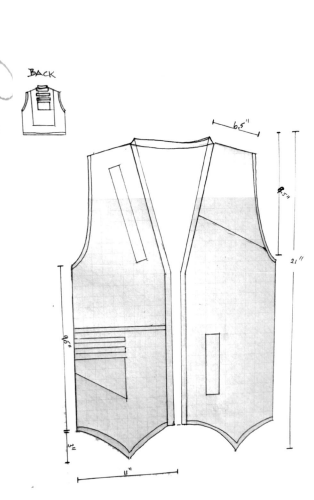

BACK

6.5"

21"

9.5"

3"

4"

Row 75: P to last 6 st., seed 6 st.
Repeat these 5 rows. 2 more times
Row 86: Seed 6 st., K4, K4 (C2); with C1,K2 TOG, K to end of row(29 st.).
Row 87: P15, P4 (C2), P4 (C1), seed 6 st.
Row 88: Seed 6 st., K4 (C1), K4 (C2), K to end of row.
Row 89: P in color pattern to last 6 st., seed 6 st.
Repeat these last two rows until you reach 21"from bottom point.
Make sure you decrease 1 st. by K2 TOG every 6 rows. Bind off but keep the 6 seed st. for the border band live and put them on a stitch holder.

Left Front:

Cast on 5 st. with C1
Follow directions for the right front up until row 12.
Row 12: M1, seed 6 st., P3 (middle stitches), seed to last st. (16 st.) (The middle st. are stockinette).
Row 13: Cast on 5 st. seed 12 st., K3, seed to end of row (21 st.).
Row 14: Cast on 5 st. seed 11 st., P5, seed to end of row (26 st.).
Row 15: Cast on 5 st. seed 15 st., K7, seed to end of row (31 st.).
Row 16: Cast on 5 st. seed 14 st., P9, seed to end of row (36 st.).
Row 17: Cast on 4 st. seed 17 st., K 11, seed to end of row (40 st.).
Row 18: Seed 11 st., P13 st., seed to end of row.
Row 19: Seed 15 st., K15 st., seed to last 6 st., seed 6 st.
Row 20: Seed 9 st., P17, seed to end of row,
Row 21: Seed13 st., K19, seed to last 6 st., seed 6 st.
Row 22: Seed 6 st. (this is your border band), P 21, seed to end of row.
Row 23: Seed 11 s., K 23, seed to last 6 st., seed 6 st.
Row 24: Seed 6 st., P25, seed to end of row.
Row 25: Seed 7 st., K27, seed 6 st.
Row 26: Seed 6 st., P29, seed to end of row.
Row 27: Seed 3 st., K 31, seed 6 st.
Row 28: Seed 6 st., P34
Row 29: K34, seed 6 st.
Repeat these last 2 rows, 2 more times. (4 rows)
Row 34: K26, K4 with C2, (stranded) K4 (C1), seed 6 st.
Row 35: Seed 6 st., P4, P4 (C2), P to end of row.
Repeat these last 2 rows, 12 more times (24 rows).
(You should now have 10" from the bottom point).
Row 60: K to last 6 st., seed 6 st. All in C1
Row 61: Seed 6, P to end of row.
Repeat these last 2 rows, 3 more times. (6 rows)
This is the point where you decrease for the armhole.
You should now have 12" from the bottom point, 9.5" from the seam side
Row 68: Bind off 7 st., K to last 6 st., seed 6 st.
Decrease for the V-Neck. These are done in the center

of the front panel, and decreases are done every 6 rows. Here is also the one short row for the border band to allow for the bend in the garment.

Row 69: (short row) Seed 6 st., turn, seed 6 st. back.

Row 70: Seed 6 st., P8, P2 TOG, P to end of row (decrease 1 st. every 6 rows).

Row 71: K to last 6 st., seed 6 st.

Row 72: Seed 6 st., P to end of row.

Next you introduce C2, for the diagonal color change.

Row 73: K1(2), K to last 6 st., seed 6 st. (C1).

Row 74: Seed 6 st., P to last 2 st. P2 (C2).

Row 75: K3 (C2), K to last 6 st., seed 6 st. (C1).

Row 76: Seed 6 st., P8, P2 TOG, P to last 4 st. P4 (C2) (31 st.).

Row 77: K5 (C2), K to last 6 st., seed 6 st. (C1).

Row 78: Seed 6 st., P to last 6 st., P 6 st (C2).

Row 79: K7 (C2), K (with C1) to last 6 st., seed 6 st.

Row 80: Seed 6 st., P to last 8 st., P 8 (C2).

Row 81: K9 (C2), K to last 6 st., seed 6 st.

Row 82: Seed 6 st., P2 TOG, P5, P10 (C2).

Row 83: K11 (C2), K13 (with C1), seed 6 st.

Row 84: Seed 6 st., P to last 12 st., P 12 (C2).

Row 85: K13 (C2), K (with C1) to last 6 st., seed 6 st.

Row 86: Seed 6 st., P10, P14 (C2).

Row 87: K 15,(C2), K to last 6 st. Seed 6.

Row 88: Seed 6 st., P8, P2 TOG (C2), P to end (29 st.).

Row 89, K16, (C2), K7, seed 6 st.

Row 90: Seed 6 st., P7, with C2 P to end of row.

Row 91: K18 (C2), K5, seed 6 st.

Row 92: Seed 6 st., P4 with C2, P to end of row.

Row 93: K20, (C2), K3, Seed 6.

Row 94: Seed 6 st., P2, with C2 P6, P2 TOG, P to end of row.

Row 95: K20 (C2), with C1 K1, seed 6 st.

Row 96: Seed 6 st.(C1), with C2 P to end of row.

Continue with C1 for your seeded border band and C2 as the body of the front, decreasing every 6 rows. You are now at 17".

Continue in this color pattern for another 4" (remember to decrease every 6 rows) until you have 21" total length from the bottom point.

You should have 24 st. left (6 seed st. and 18 regular st.)

Bind off 18 regular st. and put the 6 seed st. on a stitch holder.

Sew shoulders and side seam together.

Finishing the neck band:

Pick up the 6 seed st. on the right side of the front and knit and purl to the middle, while picking up st. from the back. (Make sure not to increase the 6 st.) Knit one stitch of the band and one stitch of the body together. Do the same for the left side and sew the band together in the middle.

Armhole edging:

Sew the shoulder and the side seams of the vest.

With #6 needle pick up 70 st. around the armhole. Don't make a circle but knit back and forth. The ends will be sewn to the square armhole bottom.

You will create a deeper (broader) band in the back than in the front.

With the RS facing you, knit one row. You are now at the back of the armhole. Working in seed st. knit 35 st. to the top of the shoulder. Turn and seed back.

Next 2 rows work in seed st. the whole way (70 st.) You are now at the back again.

Work in seed st. for 35 st., turn and seed back.

Next row work in seed st. the whole way (70 st.).

Next row bind off.

Use the same process for the other armhole, making sure that the deeper (broader) band is in the back.

Finishing:

Weave in all loose ends and gently block the vest.

The easiest way to strand one color behind another is to hold one color in each hand.

Wave West Vest

This vest was created for the first fashion show that launched Fibershed. Models walked on a catwalk of straw bales, showing off the most wonderful clothing sourced and made within some eighty miles from West Marin.

This design came to me when I read Lynn Barr's Reversible Knitting. Her book opened my eyes to all the possibilities of knitting beyond the ordinary.

Skill level:
Experienced

Measurements:
The size given is a medium to large. Only one size is given

Finished sizes:
Top to bottom: 20"
Bottom to sleeve: 8"
Sleeve bottom to shoulder: 10"
Right front bottom width: 9"
Top width: 22"
Collar: 1"

Yarns:
Bo-Rage mill-spun, 100% Shetland, heavy worsted 2 ply, 1000 yds.
Equivalent commercial yard is Brown Sheep Lamb's Pride worsted weight.

Needles:
Needle size # 8 or size to obtain gauge. Main needle
One set of #8 double point needle

Gauge:
4 sts. = 1 inch
5 rows = 1 inch

General note:
This vest is knit from top to bottom. You start with a provisional cast on, because the shoulder ribs and collar are knit afterwards. When finished, the fronts and back are stitched together at the shoulders. For the front diagonal rib panel, the stitches are picked up and knit in short rows creating the distinctive bias.

Right front:

Cast on 49 stitches with a provisional CO

Row 1: WS, K

Row 2: P

Rows 3 & 4: Repeat rows 1 & 2.

Row 5: P

Row 6: K

Rows 7 & 8: Repeat rows 5 & 6.

Rows 9-12: Repeat rows 1-4.

Rows 13-16: Repeat rows 5-8.

Rows 17-20: Repeat rows 1-4 ending on WS.

Next start rib pattern on row 21

Row 21: (WS) P6, K4, P7, K4, P7, K4, P7, K4, P6

Row 22: K6, P4, K7, P4, K7, P4, K7, P4, K6

Repeat rows 21 & 22 for a total of 17 rows ending on RS.

Next knit the wave pattern – See instructions for right front wave patterns below:

After you have finished the wave pattern, continue in rib pattern for another 5.5 inches or until piece measures 11". The last row should be on the RS.

Right front armhole bind off:

With RS facing, bind off 10 stitches for armhole. Continue in the rib pattern on the remaining 39 sts. for 4 more inches. At this point you will start to decrease the number of stitches in the ribs to create narrower ribs.

Begin decreases for right front panel as follows:

Row 1: (RS) K7, P4, K5, K2 TOG, P4, K5, K2 TOG, P4, K6 (37 sts)

Row 2: Knit the knits and purl the purls continuing with the rib pattern.

Row 3-5: Repeat row 2.

Row 6: WS P6, K2, K2 TOG, P6, K2, K2 TOG, P6, K2, K2 TOG, P7 (34 sts)

Rows 7-10: Repeat row 2.

Row 11: RS K7, P3, SSK, K4, P3, SSK, K4, P3, K6 (32 sts)

Rows 12-15: Repeat row 2.

Row 16: WS P4, P2 TOG, K3, P5, K3, P5, K3, SSP, P5 (30 sts)

Rows 17-20: Repeat row 2.

Row 21: RS K6, P3, K3, K2tog, P3, K3, K2tog, P3, K5 (28 sts)

Rows 22-25: Repeat row 2.

Row 26: WS P5, K1, K2 TOG, P4, K1, K2 TOG, P4, K1, K2 TOG, P6 (26 sts)

Rows 27-30: Repeat row 2.

Row 31: RS K6, P2, K4, P2, K4, P2, K2 TOG, K2 (23 sts)

Rows 32-34: Repeat row 2.

Rows 35: RS K6, P2, K4, P2, K4, P2, K2 TOG, K1 (22 sts)

Repeat row 2 until piece measures 22".

With RS facing, bind off loosely in pattern.

Left front:

The left front will be a mirror image of the right front.

Follow instruction for right front until it is time to do the wave pattern. The wave pattern is a reverse of the right front. Follow instructions for left front wave pattern below. As with right front, continue knitting in pattern for 4 more inches until the piece measures 11".

Left front armhole bind off:

With WS facing, bind off 10 sts. Continue to end of row.

Continue in pattern for the remaining 39 sts for 4".

Knit one row in pattern.

Begin left front decreases starting on the RS:

Row 1: (RS) K6, P4, K5, K2 TOG, P4, K5, K2 TOG, P4, K7 (37 sts)

Row 2: Knit the knits and purl the purls continuing with the rib pattern.

Rows 3-5: Repeat row 2.

Row 6: WS P7, K2, K2 TOG, P6, K2, K2 TOG, P6, K2, K2 TOG, P6 (34 sts)

Rows 7-10: Repeat row 2.

Row 11: RS K6, P3, SSK, K4, P3, SSK, K4, P3, K7 (32 sts)

Rows 12-15: Repeat row 2.

Row 16: WS P5, P2 TOG, K3, P5, K3, P5, K3, SSP, P4 (30 sts)

Rows 17-20: Repeat row 2.

Row 21: RS K5, P3, K3, K2 TOG, P3, K3, K2 TOG, P3, K6 (28 sts)

Rows 22-25: Repeat row 2.

Row 26: WS P6, K1, K2 TOG, P4, K1, K2 TOG, P4, K1, K2 TOG, P5 (25 sts)

Rows 27-30: Repeat row 2.

Row 31: RS K5,K2 TOG, P2, K4, P2, K4, P2, K2 TOG, K2

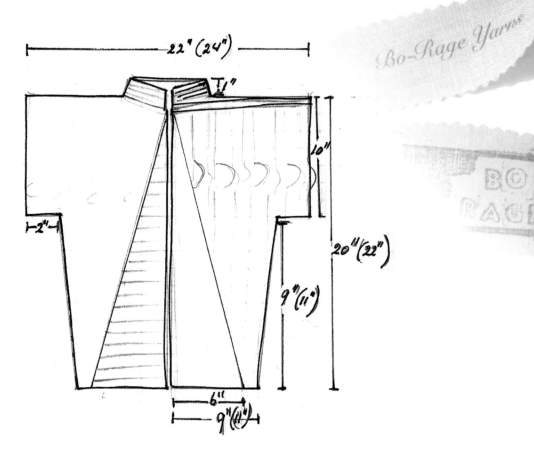

(23 sts)

Rows 32-34: Repeat Row 2.

Rows 35: RS K1 K2 TOG, P2, K4, P2, K4, P2, K6 (22 sts)

Repeat row 2 until piece measures 22".

With RS facing, bind off loosely in pattern.

Back:

Cast on 82 sts. with a provisional CO.

Follow left and right front instructions for collar ending with row 20 on WS.

Row 21: WS, P6, K4, P7, K4, P7, K4, P7, K4, P7, K4, P7, K4, P7, K4, P6

Row 22: RS, K6, P4, K7, P4, K7, P4, K7, P4, K7, P4, K7, P4, K7, P4, K6

Repeat rows 21 & 22 for 16 more rows.

Next do the wave pattern as follows:

Knit the fold #2 until you reach the middle of the row. Then knit fold #1 for rest of row.

Knit rib pattern for 9 rows.

Knit fold #1 until you reach the middle of the row.

Knit fold #2 for rest of row.

After completing the wave pattern, continue in rib pattern for 5.5 inches or until piece measures 11".

Armholes bind off:

Next, with RS facing, bind off 10 stitches for armhole. Knit remaining 72 stitches in pattern. Next, with WS facing bind off 10 stitches. Knit remaining 62 sts in pattern.

Continue in rib pattern on the remaining 62 stitches until piece measures 22".

Bind off loosely in pattern.

Wave pattern instructions:
The wave pattern is done using two versions of the fold pattern:

Fold pattern #1:
With RS facing, rotate work forward so WS is showing and knitting is above needle.

Using a double pointed needle, PU the last four stitches of the first rib on the WS of the piece, 6 rows below the current row.

Rotate work back so RS is facing and hold the DP behind and next to the main needle. Knit the stitches on the main needle and the DP together. You are knitting the first st. on the main needle with the first stitch on the DP. Knit together the remaining sts. on DP with the next 3 sts on the main needle. The work on the DP gets pulled up and forward.

Knit remaining sts. in rib pattern. (In case of 6 st rib this will be 2 sts., and in the case of 7 st rib this will be 3 sts) Note: Between each rib you will P4.
Repeat the #1 fold stitch with the remaining 4 ribs.
You do not increase any stitches.
Next knit 9 rows in the rib pattern, then do a reverse fold which will complete the wave.

Fold pattern #2:
This fold will change the direction, thus creating the wave.
With RS facing, rotate work forward so WS is showing and knitting is above needle.
Using a double point needle, PU the first four stitches of the first rib on the WS of the piece, 6 rows below the current row.

Rotate work back so RS is facing and hold the DP behind and next to the main needle. Knit the first 2 or 3 stitches on the main needle (depending on if it is a 6 or 7 st rib.) Then knit the remaining 4 sts together with the 4 stitches on the main needle with the sts on the DP. Knit remaining sts in rib pattern.
Repeat this #2 fold stitch with the remaining 4 ribs.

Note: switching from fold #1 to fold #2 creates the wave pattern.

Left front side wave pattern:
Knit the #1 fold pattern first and the #2 pattern second.

Right front side wave pattern:
Knit the #2 fold pattern first and the #1 pattern second.

Row 9: K2, P2, K2, P2, K2, P2, K2, P2, K2 W&T (20 st.)

You have completed about ¼ of the 82 sts. The horizontal rib pattern is well established.

Continue in this pattern, advancing four stitches every odd numbered row for all 82 sts then you have reached the collar of the right front vest.

Left front diagonal panel (mirror image of right front diagonal panel):

With RS facing PU 82 stitches along right side of left front piece.

RS facing and starting at the top, knit one row.

With WS facing begin the short rows. The rib pattern will be formed in the same manner as the right front except all knits will be purls and all purls will be knits.

Front diagonal panels:

Right front diagonal panel:

With RS facing, PU 82 sts along left side of front panel.

WS facing, purl one row.

With RS facing, starting at the bottom, begin the short rows. When complete, this will create the horizontal ribbed front diagonal panel.

Row 1: K2, P2, W&T

Rows 2: Knit back to beginning (ie. bottom of piece) keeping in the rib pattern you have started in row 1 (ie: knit the knits and purl the purls)

Row 3: K2, P2, K2, P2 W&T (8 st.)

Row 4: Repeat row 2 for all even numbered rows.

Row 5: K2, P2, K2, P2, K2, P2 W&T (12 st.)

Row 7: K2, P2, K2, P2, K2, P2, K2, P2 W&T (16 st.)

Row 1: P2, K2, W&T

Rows 2: Knit back to beginning (ie: bottom of piece) keeping in the rib pattern you have started in row 1 (ie: knit the knits and purl the purls).

Row 3: P2, K2, P2, K2, P2 W&T (8 st.)

Row 4: Repeat row 2 for all even numbered rows.

Row 5: P2, K2, P2, K2, P2, K2, W&T (12 st.)

Row 7: P2, K2, P2, K2, P2, K2, P2, K2 W&T (16 st.)

Row 9: P2, K2, P2, K2, P2, K2, P2, K2, P2, K2 W&T (20 st.)

You have completed about ¼ of the 82 sts. The horizontal rib pattern is well established.

Continue in this pattern, advancing four stitches every odd numbered row, for all 82 sts and you have reached the collar at the top of the left front vest.

Bind off in pattern loosely for all 82 stitches.

NECK:

Back of neck:

PU the 82 sts that were provisionally CO at top of back. With RS facing you and starting at the armhole side, bind off 25 sts. knitwise for the right shoulder leaving 57 sts. Knit to end of row. With WS facing, bind off 25 sts. purlwise for the left shoulder. There are 32 sts. remaining on the needle.

Left front of neck:

PU the 49 sts CO provisionally at top of left front. With RS facing you and starting at the armhole side, bind off 25 sts knitwise. Knit to end of row. There will be 24 sts remaining on needle.

Right front of neck:

PU the 49 sts that were provisionally CO at top of right front. With WS facing you and starting at the armhole side, bind off 25 sts purlwise. Purl to end of row. There will be 24 stitches remaining on needle.

Sew shoulder seams together.

Collar:

With WS facing purl the 24 sts from right front, purl the 32 sts from back and purl the 24 sts from left front.

Continue in pattern for 6 rows as follows:

Row 1: Knit

Row 2: Purl

Row 3: Purl

Row 4: Knit

Row 5: Purl

Row 6: Knit back to beginning (i.e., bottom of piece) keeping in the rib pattern you have started in

Bind off knit-wise.

Finishing:

Weave in all loose ends and gently block the vest.

Drake's Crown

This hat (or beret) is rather flat and sits straight on your head. The angora rabbit yarn is fluffy and soft and gives the hat band a halo effect.

Skill level:
Easy to intermediate

Finished size:
9" Diameter at the widest point
7" From top to bottom

Yarn:
Bo-Rage hand-spun angora rabbit, single, sports weight. approx. 75 yards
Bo-Rage mill-spun, 2 ply worsted weight approx. 75 yards

Needles:
6 24" circular needle or needle size to obtain gauge. Main needle
6 double pointed needles
4 24" circular needles for the hat band

Notions:
Tapestry needle
Stitch markers
Tape measure
Crochet hook

Gauge:
4 st = 1 inch
6 rows = 1 inch

Hat band:
With the circular #4 needle and C1, cast on 100 st.
Place marker at beginning of the row. and join.
K2, P2 in rib st. for 16 rows, approx. 2.5".

Change to needle size #6.
Next row: K
Next row: P
Next row: P, increase 1 st. every 10 st. *M1, P10*, repeat to end of row. (110 st.)
Next 6 rows: P without increases.
Next row: P, decrease 1 st. every 10 st. *P2 TOG, P10* repeat to end off row. (100 st.)
Change yarns to C2. (mill-spun)
You are now starting the crown.
Knit all rows and decrease as follows:
At the beginning of the row (at the place marker), K2 TOG, K10, repeat to end of row.
Next row: K
Next row: K2 TOG, K9, repeat to end of row.
Next row: K
Continue in this manner until you have 6 st. left.
At some point it will be easier to use double pointed needles.

Finishing:
Cut thread and with a crochet hook pull the thread through the remaining stitches.
Weave in all loose ends.

Woolscapes

Inverness Cardigan

This pattern is knit in panels, bottom to top. The back panel is a straight rectangle. The front panels are shaped to accommodate the sleeve openings. The sleeves are knit from the shoulder to the wrist by picking up stitches at the arm openings. To loosen the bound off edges, you may want to bind off with a larger size needle. The entire sweater is written line by line.

Skill level:
Difficult

Measurements:
Size given is a medium. Only one size is available.

Finished size:
Length of sweater body is 22 ½" – 23 ½"
Width of sweater body is 37"- 39 ½"
Length of sleeve is 22-23"

Yarn:
Worsted weight wool, 7 skeins @ 200 yards or 1400 yards total.

Needles:
Size # 8 or needle size to obtain the gauge. Main needle

Size #6 needle, or needle size two sizes smaller than main needle

Notions:
Cable needle
Tapestry needle
Measuring tape

Gauge:
4 stitches = 1 inch
5.5 Rows = 1 inch

Back:
CO 64 stitches on the smaller size needle and work as below until piece measures 2". Then switch to main needle.

Row 1: Knit
Row 2: Purl
Row 3: Seed 6 (S6), PM, *P4, K4*, Repeat **5 more times, P4, PM, S6
Row 4: S6, *K4, P4*, repeat ** 5 more times, K4, S6
Row 5: S6, *P4, C4B (K2 onto cn and hold in back, K2, K2 from cn)*, repeat ** 5 more times, P4, S6

Row 6: S6, *K4, P4*, repeat **5 X, K4, S6. From here on work in pattern for all even numbered rows.

Rows 7-14: Repeat rows 3-6 three times until piece measures 2".

Note that the cable pattern now changes from every 2 rows to every 4 rows.

Change to larger size needle.

Row 15: S6, *P4, C4B*, repeat** five more times, P4, S6

Row 17: S6, *P4, K4*, repeat ** five more times, P4, S6

Next 20 rows: CIP until piece measures 7".

Next increase the purl columns and decrease the knit columns as follows:

Row 39: (RS) S6, P5, *K2, P6*, repeat** 4 more times, K2, P5, S6

Now that the increase and decrease of the columns have occurred, CIP until piece measures 9" (about row 50).

Row 51: (RS), S6, P5, K2, P6, K2, P6, K2, P2, K2(these are the 2 center sts), P2, K2, P6, K2, P6, K2, P5, S6.

Row 53: Repeat row 51.

Next start the traveling cables:

Row: 55: S6, P5, K2, P6, K2, P6, K2, C3B#1 (P1 onto cn and hold in back, K2, P1 from cn), C3F#1(K2 onto cn

and hold in front, P1, K2 from cn), K2, P6, K2, P6, K2, P5, S6

Row 57: S6, P5, K2, P6, K2, P6, C4B, P2, C4F, P6, K2, P6, K2, P5, S6

Row 59: S6, P5, K2, P6, K2, P4, C4PB (P2 onto cn and hold in back, k2, p2 from cn), K2, P2, K2, C4KF (knit 2 onto cn and hold in front, P2, K2 from cn), P4, K2, P6, K2, P5, S6

Row 61: S6, P5, K2, P6, K2, P2, C4PB, P2, K2, P2, K2, P2, C4KF, P2, K2, P6, K2, P5, S6

Row 63: S6, P5, K2, P6, K2, C4PB, P4, K2, P2, K2, P4, C4KF, K2, P6, K2, P5, S6

Row 65: S6, P5, K2, P6, C4B, P6, K2, P2, K2, P6, C4F, P6, K2, P5, S6

Row 67: S6, P5, K2, C4PB, K2, P6, K2, P2 K2, P6, K2, C4KF, P4, K2, P5, S6

Row 69: S6,P5, K2, P2, C4PB, P2, k2, P6, K2, P2, K2, P6, K2, P2, C4KF, P2, K2, P5, S6

Row 71: S6, P5, K2, C4PB, P4, K2, P6, K2, P2, K2, P6, K2, P4, C4KF, K2, P5, S6

Start of another cross back cable:

Row 73: S6, P5, C4B, P6, K2, P4, C4PB, P2, C4KF, P4, K2, P6, C4F, P5, S6

Row 75: S6, P3, C4PB, K2, P6, K2, P2, C4PB, K2, P2, K2, C4KF, P2, K2, P6, K2 C4KF, P3, S6

Row 77: S6, P1, C4PB, P2, K2, P6, K2, C4PB, P2, K2,P2,

K2, P2, C4KF, K2, P6, K2, P2, C4KF, P1, S6

Row 79: S6, C4PB, P3, K2, P6, C4B, P4, K2, P2, K2, P4, C4F, P6, K2, P3, C4KF, S6

Row 81: S6, K1, P6, K2, P4, C4PB, K2, P4, K2, P2, K2, P4, K2, C4KF, K2, P4, K2, P6, K1, S6

Row 83: S6, K1, P6, K2, P2, C4PB, P2, K2, P4, K2, P2, K2, P4, K2, P2, C4KF, P2, K2, P6, K1, S6

Row 85: S6, K1, P6, K2, C4PB, P4, K2, P4, K2, P2, K2, P4, K2, P4, C4KF, K2, P6, K1, S6

Row 87: S6, K1, P6, C4B, P6, K2, p4, K2, P2, K2, P4, K2, P6, C4F, P6, K1, S6

Row 89: S6, K1, P4, C4PB, K2, P6, K2, P4, K2, P2, K2, P4, K2, P6, K2, C4KF, P4, K1, S6

Row 91: S6, K1, P2, C4PB, P2, K2, P6, K2, P2, C4PB, P2, C4KF, P2, K2, P6, K2, P2, C4KF, P2, K1, S6

Row 93: S6, K1, C4PB, P4, K2, P6, K2, C4PB, P6, C4KF, K2, P6, K2, P4, C4KF, K1, S6

Row 95: S6, C3B#2, P6, K2, P6, C4B, P10, C4F, P6, K2, P6, C3F#2, S6

Row 97: S6, C2B (P1 onto cn and hold in back, K1, P1 from cn) , P7, K2, P4, C4BP, K2, P4, K2, P4, K2, C4FK, P4, K2, P7, C2F(K1 onto cn and hold in front, P1, K1 from cn), S6

Row 99: S6, K1, P8, K2, P4, K2, P2, K2, P2, C3PB(P2 onto cn and hold in back, k1, p2 from cn), C3KF (K1 onto cn and hold in front, P2, K1 from cn), P2, K2, P2, K2, P4, K2, P8, K1, S6

Row: 101: S6, K1, P8, K2, P4, K2, P2, K2, P1, TSL(K1 onto cn and hold in front, P1, K1 from cn), P4, TSR(P1 onto cn and hold in back, K1, P1 from cn) P1, K2, P2, K2, P4, K2, P8, K1, S6

Row 103: S6, K1, P8, K2, P4, C4KF, K2, P1, K1, P6, K1, P1, K2, C4PB, P4, K2, P8, K1, S6

Row 105: S6, K1, P8, K2, P6, C4F, P1, TSR, P4, TSL, P1, C4B, P6, K2, P8, K1, S6

Row 107: S6, K1, P8, K2, P6, K4, P2, TSR, P2, TSL, P2, K4, P6, K2, P8, K1, S6

Row 109: S6, K1, P8, K2, P6, K2, C3KF, P2, K1,P2, K1, P2 , C3PB, K2, P6,P2 P8, K1, S6

Row 111: S6, K1, P8, K2, P6, K2, C3KF, P1, C2B, C2F, P1, C3PB, K2, P6, K2, P8, K1, S6

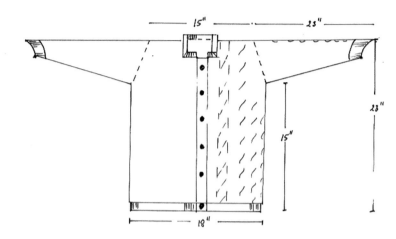

Row 113: S6, K1, P8, K2, P6, K2, P2, K2, P2, K2, P2, K2, P2, K2, P6, K2, P8, K1, S6

Row 115: S6, K1, P8, K2, P6, K2, P2, K2, P2, K2, P2, K2, P2, K2, P6, K2, P8, K1, S6

Row 117: S6, K1, P8, K2, P6, K2, P2, C4FK, K2, C4BP, P2, K2, P6, K2, P8, K1, S6

Row 119: S6, K1, P8, K2, P6, K2, P4, C3F#2 (K2 onto cn and hold in front, K1, K2 from cn, C3B#2 (K1 onto cn and hold in back, K2, k1 from cn), P4, K2, P6, K2, P8, K1, S6

Row 121: S6, K1, P8, K2, P6, K2, P5, K4, P5, K2, P6, K2, P8, K1, S6

Row 123: S6, K1, P8, K2, P6, K2, P5, C2F, C2B, P5, K2, P6, K2, P8, K1, S6

Row 125: S6, K1, P8, K2, P6, K2, P6, K2, P6, K2, P6, K2, P8, K1, S6

Rows 127 – 133: Repeat rows 125 and 126 five times. Piece should measure about 23 ½"

Bind off all 64 sts.

Right Front:

Starting with the smaller size needles cast on 50 sts.

Row 1: Knit

Row 2: Purl

Row 3: RS, S6, K8, *P4, K4*, repeat ** 3 more times, P4

Row 4: WS, Knit the knits and purl the purls as follows:*K4, P4*, repeat ** 3 more times, K4, P8, S6

Repeat this row of knitting the knits and purling the purls for all subsequent even numbered rows while maintaining the Seed 6 pattern.

Row 5: S6, TSL, K6, *P4, C4F*, repeat ** three more times, P4

Row 7: S6, K1, TSL, K5, *P4, C4F*, repeat** 3 more times, P4

Row 9: S6, K2, TSL, K4, *P3, C4F*, repeat ** 3 more times, P4

Change to larger size needles.

From here on the C4F cable will be done every 4 rows.

Row 11: S6, K3, TSL, K3, *P4, K4*, repeat ** 3 more times, P4

Row 13: S6, K4, TSL, K2, *P4, C4F*, repeat ** 3 more times, P4

Row 15: S6, K5, TSL, K1, CIP

Row 17: S6, K6, TSL, *P4, C4F*, repeat ** three more times, P4

Row 19: S6, K8, CIP

Repeat rows 11-19 until piece measures 11". Remember to maintain the TSL and the C4F. From here, eliminate the cable under the arm on the left side of piece.

Row 65-69: CIP

Row 70: WS, Bind off 8sts, CIP, ending with K8. (42sts)

Rows 71-73: CIP

Row 74: Bind off 2sts, CIP (40sts)

Row 75: S6, TS pat, P4, K4, P4, K16 (40sts)

Row 77: S6, TS pat., P4, C4F, P4, SSK, K12 (39sts)

Row 79: S6, TS pat, P4, K4, P4, SSK, K11 (38sts)

Row 80: CIP. Note: The number of knit sts at end of row will decrease by one on every odd numbered row

until 26 stitches remain.

CIP on the 26 stitches until the piece measures 21-21 1/2".

The last row should match the end of the last 8st. TSL pattern. If not, continue in pattern until it matches.

Neck edge:

RS, Bind off 10sts, CIP.

On the next RS row, bind off 2sts, CIP.

CIP for 2 ½ more inches.

Bind off remaining 14 stitches at neck edge.

The total length should be approximately 23 ½".

Left front:

The left front is a mirror image of the right front. Follow directions for the right front with the following changes:

1. The traveling stitch needs to be reversed, meaning that the 8 stitch traveling stitch pattern will have a TSR.
2. The S6 will start on the left side.
3. When performing the decreases under the arm on the left, decrease by K2 TOG, (not SSK).

Row 1: Knit

Row 2: Purl

Row 3: *P4, K4,* repeat ** 3 more times, p4, K8, S6

Row 4 and all even numbered rows: Knit and purl in pattern, remembering to S6 at the beginning of row.

Row 5: *P4, C4F*, repeat** three more times, P4, K6, TSR, S6

CIP until 26 sts remain as with the right side.
Next, on the WS, bind off 10 sts in pattern.
Next, WS, bind off 2 sts.
CIP for 2 ½" more.

Bind off remaining 14 stitches at neck edge.
Sew the front and back panels together (14sts for each panel) at the shoulder. Leave the sides open.

Sleeves:
The sleeves are knit from picked up stitches at the shoulder and worked down to the wrist.

Pick up 64 sts, 32 sts from the front panel and 32 sts from the back panel: With RS facing start the pickups on the front panels where the gusset 2 sts bind off occurred. Finish the pick-ups on the back panel at about row 73 (ie: where the 2ndcross cable begins).
Rows 1-6: Knit in Stockinette St for 6 rows, starting with a knit row for 6 ½".
Now begin the cable at 6 ½".
Row 7: Knit 28 sts, C4B, C4F, Knit 28 sts
Row 8+: K and P all even numbered rows.
Row 9: Knit 26, C4B, K4, C4F, K26
Row 11: Knit 26, C4F, K4, C4B, K26
Row 13: K28, C4F, C4B, K28
Repeat these 10 rows until sleeve measures 6 ½".

Start the decreases.
Knit 2, K2 TOG at beginning of row, CIP until you reach 4 stitches from end. K2 TOG, knit 2. Repeat this decrease row every 6 rows while at the same time maintaining the 10-row cable pattern.
When sleeve measures about 12" or 54 stitches, start to decrease as above every 4 rows until there are 34 sts.

At 34 stitches and at the end of a cable circle, change needles to the smaller size.
Row 1: K11, C4F, K4, C4B, K11
Rows 2&4: P
Row 3: K13, C4F, C4B, K13
Repeat these 4 rows for 2 ½" - 3" or 3 more times.
Row 16: Bind off 5sts PW and continue in CIP
Row 14: Bind off 5sts PW and CIP
Row 15: Bind off 4sts PW and CIP
Row 16: Bind off 4sts PW and CIP
Row 17: Bind off 3sts PW and CIP
Row 16: Bind off 3sts PW and CIP
Row 17: Bind off 3sts PW and CIP
Row 18: Bind off 3sts PW and CIP
Row 19: K1, PSSO, K1
Row 19: Bind off remaining 3 sts.

Sleeve Gusset:
Pickup 10 sts where you bound off the 10 sts for the arm opening.
With WS facing and starting with a purl row, knit in stockinette stitch for 15 rows.
At row 16, decrease one st. at beginning and end of each row until there is one st. left. Pull yarn through last stitch.

Front button band:
Starting with the left front and the smaller size needle, pick up 80 sts.
K2, P2 (rib pat) for 1 ½".
Bind off loosely.
Repeat for the right front band except you will need to create 6 button holes, evenly spaced.

Neck band:
Pick up 68 sts with the smaller size needle. Seed stitch for 1". Bind off all 68 sts.

Finishing:
Sew all parts together and weave in loose ends. Block sweater carefully. Sew on buttons.

Dirndl Top

Tyrolian as well as German traditional folk costumes often have a lace-up front. The flexibility in sizing with a lace up front is easy. The front in this top is created by knitting the left part and the right part separately. Then stitches are picked up on one front for the middle section, which is knit sideways and sewn to the other front side. Then with a crocheted string the "dirndl" effect is achieved by weaving the string through the folded front panels and pulling these panels over the "insert" in the front.

Skill level:
Easy

Measurements:
One size is given. The sample is a medium. However the design is such that the front panel can be "drawn" in, so it can be made tighter or looser to fit many body shapes and sizes.

Finished size:
Chest: 17" (reined in)
Length to armhole: 11"
Armhole to shoulder: 7"
Total Length: 18"

Yarn:
Bo-Rage hand-spun Cormo from Starbuck Farm in Valley Ford, natural white. 2 ply, DK weight, 4 skeins approx. 400 Yards

Needles:
Straight or circular # 4 or correct needle size to obtain gauge. Main needle #3 for bottom band

Notions:
Stitch holders
Embroidery needle
Crochet hook
Measuring tape

Gauge:
4.5 st. = 1 inch
5.5 rows = 1 inch

Stitch pattern:
Stockinette

Back:

Cast on 60 stitches with needle #3.

Knit row one

Next row K2, P2 in rib pattern for 3″, approx. 18 rows

Change to stockinette stitch and needle #4.

Knit one row.

Purl one row.

Repeat these 2 rows for 8″ (total 11″)   Now you will decrease for the arm opening.

Shape arm opening:

Bind off 8 stitches at the beginning of the next 2 rows (each side of the panel) and continue in stockinette pattern for another 6″ (total of 17″). Now you will decrease for the neck opening.

Neck opening:

With the RS facing you, K 15 st., bind off 14 st. and K 15 st. Put the first 15 st. on a stitch holder. Work the left shoulder strap, in stockinette St. for 2 rows (or .5″).

Shoulder slant shaping:

Next row, decrease 5 st. on the LEFT arm side and work across row and back.   When you return to this side,

decrease 5 st. again and repeat again until no stitches are left.

Repeat these guidelines for the other side of the shoulder, making sure that the decreases for the shoulder slant are on the RIGHT arm side.

Left front:

Cast on 35 stitches with a provisional cast on, with needles size #4.

Knit first row. (You will do the rib pattern band after the whole front has been put together)

Work in stockinette stitch (K one row, P one row) until panel measures 8 inches from the cast on edge, ending with RS (knit side) facing you.

Next row, bind off 8 st. for the arm opening. Continue in stockinette st. for another 4″. Then decrease for the neck opening.

With the WS (purl side) facing you bind off 12 st. and continue in stockinette st for another 3″. When you reach 17″ from the bottom edge, bind off 5 st. on the arm side of the front. Repeat 2 more times, no stitches left.

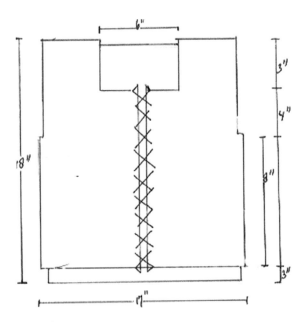

Right front:

Cast on 35 stitches with a provisional cast on. Knit base row. (You will do the rib pattern band after the whole front has been put together.)

Work in stockinette stitch until panel measures 8 inches from the cast on edge, ending with WS (purl side) facing you for the next row. Bind off 8 st. for the arm opening. Continue in stockinette st. for another 4". Then decrease for the neck opening.

With the RS (knit side) facing you, bind off 12 st. and continue in stockinette st. for another 2". When you reach 17", bind off 5 st. on the arm side of the front. Repeat 2 more times. No stitches left.

Middle front section:

This is knit sideways.

With the RS facing you and on the right side of the panel, (It is easier to pick up st. on the knit side) pick up 50 st. over the whole length of the front.

Work in stockinette stitch pattern for 5" and bind off. Sew bound off edge to the left front. Gently block all pieces and sew front and back together.

Front bottom band:

Pick up all 35 sts. from right front, 15 sts. mid section and 35 sts. left front section, for a total of 85 sts. and work in rib stitch pattern (K2,P2) for 3".
 Bind off.

Finishing:

With a crochet hook, crochet a single row around the neck opening and arm openings.

Crochet a string approx. 60 inches long and with the tapestry needle weave this string through the folded edges of the front sections, crossing over the middle insert section as shown in picture.

Weave in all loose ends and gently block the garment.

79

Ridge Hat

The ridges are created by means of a picot stitch. This stitch is YO, K2TOG. Then the rows below and above this picot row are sewn or knit together to create the ridges. The ridge rounds can be done in two different ways. The first way is to knit the picot row plus two more stockinette rows and then knit your next row together with the row that is two rows below the picot row, a method similar to a three-needle bind off, except you don't bind off. The other (easier) way is to sew the row that is two rows above and the row that is two rows below the picot row together afterwards.

Skill level:
Easy to Intermediate

Finished size:
8" from top to bottom

Yarn:
One skein of Bo-Rage mill-spun 2 ply, heavy worsted approx. 200 yards and 4 oz.
Commercial equivalent is Brown Sheep's Lambs Pride, worsted weight

Needles:
Circular 24" needle size #4 for the hat band
6 for the crown, or size to obtain gauge. Main needle
6 double pointed needles

Notions:
Stitch marker
Tapestry needle
Tape measure

Gauge:
4.5 st. = 1 inch
5 rows = 1 inch

Hat Band:
With needle size # 4 cast on 80 st. Place marker at

beginning of your row and join into the round being careful not to twist the stitches.
In K2, P2 rib stitch pattern, work 17 rows.

Body of the hat:
Change to the larger needle size for the rest of the hat.
Next knit 6 rows.
Next row is a picot row. *YO, K2 TOG.* repeat to end of row.
Next 2 rows: K. (If you are doing the three-needle method, you do it here (see explanation below*), otherwise continue the knit rows).
Next 4 more rows: K (6 rows between each picot row).
Next row is a picot row, *YO, K2 TOG* repeat to end of row.
Next 6 rows: K
Repeat picot row.
Next 2 rows: K

Crown of the hat:
Start the decreases for the crown.
Next row: *K2 TOG, K10*, repeat to end of row.
Next row: K
Next row: *K2 TOG, K9*, repeat to end of row.
Next row: K
Next row: *K 2 TOG, K8*, repeat to end of row.
Next row: K
Continue in the manner until you have 6 st. left.
Break the thread and pull through the stitches.

Finishing:
Weave in all loose ends.

If you did not do the three-needle method, create the ridges by sewing together the rows that are two rows below and two rows above the picot row.

For the three needle method:
Insert RH needle into st. four rows below the next st. on LH needle, and draw up a loop; then knit the next st. in LH needle and pass the loop over the st. just knitted.

Surface Elements

Coastal Sweater

The essence of West Marin wool is captured in this short sleeve, all hand-spun sweater. The sheep were raised in pastures just thirty miles from my home, and I know the animal that produced the curls. Martha Cant's farm is in Valley Ford, West Sonoma County, California, and the sheep graze under the redwoods. Telltale traces of the redwood needles can always be found in their wool even though Martha covers her flock of Wensleydales year round.

Skill level:
Easy to Intermediate

Measurements:
This sweater fits and looks best on a small to medium size person. Only one size is given.
This is a bulky, loose fitting sweater that is very comfortable to wear.

Finished size:
Top to bottom: 23"
Bottom width: 19"
Bottom to under arm: 10"
To width (Incl. sleeves) : 21"

Yarn:
5 skeins Bo-Rage hand-spun bulky single, approx.

16 oz., 900 yards (C1)
3 skeins Bo-Rage hand-spun bulky curls, approx. 8 oz., 200 Yards (C2)

Needles:
Needle size #15 straight or circular, or needle size to obtain gauge. Main needle
Needle size #13 for the bottom band and sleeve bands

Notions:
Tapestry needle
Measuring tape

Gauge:
3 st = 1 inch
4 rows = 1 inch

General note:
This sweater is knit from the bottom up with increases for the sleeves. The neck band and sleeve cuffs are knit from stitches picked up afterwards. Front and back panels are identical.

Front panel:
Cast on 56 st. with needle size #13.
Row 1: *K2, P2 *(in rib stitch pattern) repeat to end of row.

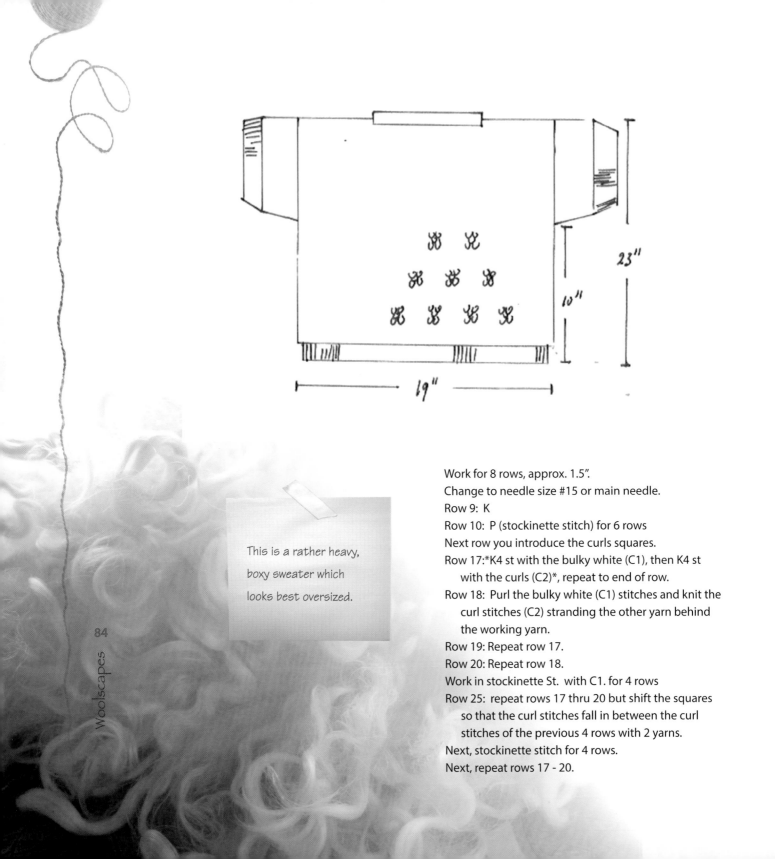

23″

10″

19″

This is a rather heavy, boxy sweater which looks best oversized.

Work for 8 rows, approx. 1.5″.

Change to needle size #15 or main needle.

Row 9: K

Row 10: P (stockinette stitch) for 6 rows

Next row you introduce the curls squares.

Row 17:*K4 st with the bulky white (C1), then K4 st with the curls (C2)*, repeat to end of row.

Row 18: Purl the bulky white (C1) stitches and knit the curl stitches (C2) stranding the other yarn behind the working yarn.

Row 19: Repeat row 17.

Row 20: Repeat row 18.

Work in stockinette St. with C1. for 4 rows

Row 25: repeat rows 17 thru 20 but shift the squares so that the curl stitches fall in between the curl stitches of the previous 4 rows with 2 yarns.

Next, stockinette stitch for 4 rows.

Next, repeat rows 17 - 20.

Continue in this manner until you have 10″.

Shaping for the sleeves:
After you have reached 10 inches, cast on10 st. on both sides for the sleeves.
Continue knitting in pattern until you have reached 21″.
Bind off.

Back panel:
Same as the front panel.

Neck band:
Sew the front and the back together at the shoulders and sides. For the head and neck, leave an opening of about 10″.
Pick up 64 stitches around the neck opening and work in rib pattern (K2, P2) for 1.5 inches.
Bind off loosely.

Sleeve cuffs:
For the sleeves, pick up 64 stitches around the arm holes and work in rib pattern (K2, P2) for 2.5 inches.
Bind off loosely.

Finishing:
Weave in any loose ends and gently block.

Hedgerow Sweater

Hedgerows are thickets of twigs, leaves and branches that go every which way, just like the rows in this sweater. You start at the bottom with a large ribbed triangle, created with short rows. Then you pick up along the hypotenuse and knit sideways, using different yarns and different stitches, creating "hedgerows" along the way.

Skill level:
Easy to Intermediate

Measurements:
This loose fitting sweater fits a medium to large size person. Only one size is given.

Finished size:
Top to bottom 22"
Bottom to sleeve 14"
Sleeve length 18"

Materials:
Bo-Rage mill-spun, heavy and light worsted, 2 ply yarn, approx. 1000 yards (5 skeins of 200 yards ea.)
The yarns used in the sample were slightly different weights. They varied from heavy worsted to light worsted. This sweater is ideal for using up leftover yarns
Colors used are:
C1 = Black

C2 = Grey
C3 = Tweed
C4 = Grey tweed
Equivalent commercial yarns would be Brown Sheep, Lamb's Pride worsted weight.

Needle size:
Circular or straight #8 or size to obtain gauge. Main needle Circular 24" #6 needle or two sizes below main needle for the wrist and bottom bands.

Notions:
Embroidery needle
Measuring tape

Gauge:
4 sts. = 1 inch
5.5 rows = 1 inch

Front panel:
(start with the triangle)
With C1 (black). Cast on 40 st.
Row 1: K
Row 2: *K2, P2* (rib pattern), repeat to end of row.

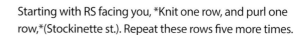

Continue in K2, P2 rib pattern for the rest of the triangle while shaping as follows:
With RS facing you: Decrease 1 st. every start of RS row (so every 2 rows) until you have no st. left. You should have 20 ribs on the bottom and zero on the top. You should have approx. 20" on the longest (underarm) straight side.

Now you start knitting sideways.
Pick up 72 stitches along the leaning side of the triangle (the hypotenuse). Don't knit the stitches as you pick them up. With the RS facing you, and the triangle's sharpest point on your left hand and the bottom of the triangle on your right hand, with C2 (Grey), knit 1 row. You are now at the top of the triangle. Turn.
Then start short rows: K2, turn, K2
K4, turn, K4
K6, turn, K6 etc. until you reach the bottom of the triangle and all 72 st. are worked.
Knit 9 more full rows.
Change to C3 (Tweed): *K2, P2* repeat to end of row. Continue in rib stitch pattern for 3 more inches.
Change to C1 (Black): Next you will create a vertical rib pattern. 5 rows stockinette st. knit side facing you and 5 rows stockinette st. purl side facing you as follows:

Starting with RS facing you, *Knit one row, and purl one row,*(Stockinette st.). Repeat these rows five more times.

Then switch so the purl side of the vertical rib is facing the RS. Create 6 ribs this way.
Change to C2 (Grey) garter st. for 10 rows. Then with the same color start the basket st., K4, P4 in columns for 4 rows, then switch and P4, K4 in columns for 4 rows. Repeat for total of 20 rows (approx. 5").
Bind off.

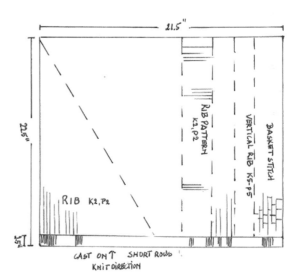

Woolscapes

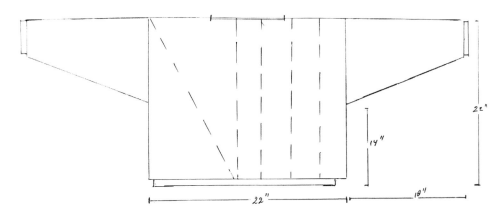

Back panel:

Repeat the directions for the front panel. You can use the same yarns or vary them according to your taste. Sew the 2 panels together at the shoulders (approx.

8") and sides approx. 11" leaving openings for neck and sleeves.

Sleeves:

These can be knit circularly or with straight needles. If using circular needles and working in the round, make sure you mark the beginning and end of your circle, because that is where the decreases will happen. With C4 (Grey Tweed) pick up 64 st. around the arm opening.

K and P 12 rows (stockinette st.) then reduce 1 st. each side (2 stitches) every other row.

At row 18, reduce 1 st. each side every 4 rows.

At row 66, (34 st. left) stop the decreases and continue in stockinette st.

At row 80, change to another color yarn and start K2, P2 rib pattern for the cuffs. Make the cuff approx. 2" long.

Bind off.

Bottom band:

For the FRONT bottom band: With Needle size #6, and with C4 (Grey Tweed) pick up 96 st. and knit the bottom band in K2, P2 rib pattern for 2.5".

Bind off.

Repeat for the back bottom band.

Finishing:

Weave in all loose ends and lightly block the garment.

The Palomarin Sweater

Just north of Bolinas is a hiking trail called the Palomarin Trailhead. This narrow path leads over the ocean cliffs to the Alamere Falls. It is a long, exposed hike with a most rewarding endpoint. This large boatneck sweater would be the ideal garment on the way back when the sun is setting and the chilly breezes blow in from the ocean.

Skill:
Beginner to intermediate

Measurements:
This is a medium size sweater. It can be made larger by using thicker yarn and needles or made smaller by using thinner yarn and thinner needles.

Finished size:
Total length: 21"
Total width: 19"
Sleeve length: 17"
Bottom to sleeve: 11"

Yarn:
Bo-Rage Mill-spun, heavy worsted 2 ply:
2 skeins (400 yards) (8 oz) Bo-Rage Mill-spun, light grey
1 skein (200 yards, 4 oz) Bo- Rage Mill-spun, dark grey
1/2 skein (100 yards, 2 oz) Bo-Rage Mill-spun, white

1/2 skein (100 yards, 2 oz) Bo-Rage Mill-spun light brown
Commercial available equivalent yarn is Brown Sheep Lamb's Pride worsted weight.

Colors:
C1 = light grey
C2 = white
C3 = light brown
C4 = dark grey

Needles:
#8 main needle, or needle size to obtain the gauge.
Main needle
#6 needle for top, bottom and sleeve bands

Notions:
Tapestry needle
Measuring tape

Gauge:
4 st. = 1 inch
6 st. = 1 inch

For the side panels you pick up stitches under the arm opening and knit them in stockinette st. sideways. The sleeves are 3/4 length.

Front panel (and back panel):

Cast on 60 st. with Needle #6 (C1).

K2, P2 repeat to end of row.

Repeat in rib pattern for 2" (approx. 12 rows). Change to Needle size #8.

Row 13: *K2 TOG, YO,* repeat to end of row

Row 14: P

Row 15: (with C2) K4, (with C1) K1, *YO, K2 TOG*, repeat to end of row.

Row 16: P

Row 17: (with C1) K6, *YO, K2 TOG*, repeat to end of row.

Row 18: (with C1) P to last 6 st., (with C2) P6.

Row 19: (With C2) K8, (with C1) K1, *YO, K2 TOG*, repeat to last st., K1.

Row 20: P

Row 21: (with C1) K12, *YO, K2 TOG*, repeat to end of row.

Row 22: (with C1) P to last 12 st., (with C2) P12.

Row 23: (with C2) K14, (with C1) K1, *YO, K2 TOG*, repeat to last st., K1.

Row 24: P

Row 25: (with C1) K18, *YO, K2 TOG*, repeat to end of row.

Row 26: (with C1) P to last 18 st., (with C2) P18.

Row 27: (with C2) K22, (with C1) K1, *YO, K2 TOG*, repeat to last st., K1.

Row 28: P

Row 29: (with C1) K26, *YO, K2 TOG*, repeat to end of row.

Row 30: (with C1) P to last 26, (with C2) P26.

Row 31: (with C2) K30, (with C1) K1, *YO, K2 TOG* repeat to last st., K1.

Row 32: P

Row 33: (with C1) K34, *YO, K2 TOG*, repeat to end of row.

Row 34: (with C1) P to last 34 st., (with C2) P34.

Woolscapes

Stitch patterns:

Stockinette stitch

YO, K2 TOG.

K2, P2 rib pattern for bands

General note:

This sweater is knit from top to bottom and in panels. You knit the front and back panels first, then the side panels and then the sleeves. Front and back panels are identical.

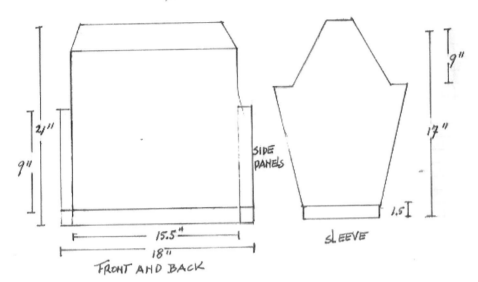

DALOMARIN SWEATER

SIDE PANELS

2"

9"

15.5"

18"

FRONT AND BACK

9"

17"

1.5

SLEEVE

Row 35: (with C2) K38, (with C1) K1, *YO, K2 TOG*, repeat to last st., K1.
Row 36: P
Row 37: (with C1) K42, *YO, K2 TOG*, repeat to end of row.
Row 38: (with C1) P to last 42 st., (with C2) P42.
Row 39: (with C2) K46, (with C1) K1, *YO, K2 TOG)*,repeat to last st. K1.
Row 40: P
Row 41: (with C1) K50, *YO, K2 TOG*, repeat to end of row.
Row 42: (with C1) P to last 50 st., (with C2) P50.
Row 43: (with C2) K54, (with C1) *YO, K2 TOG*, repeat to last st., K1.
Row 44: P
Row 45: (with C1) K58, *YO, K2 TOG*, repeat to end of row.
Row 46: (with C1) P2, (with C2) P58.
Row 47: (with C2) K
Row 48: (with C2) P
Row 49: (with C1) K
Row 50: (with C1) P

Repeat these last 4 rows once.
Here change color. Keep working with C1 (light grey), but change C2 to C3 (brown).
Row 55: (with C3) K
Row 56: (with C1) P
Row 57: (with C1) K
Row 58: (with C3) P
Row 59: (with C3) K
Row 60: (with C1) P
Repeat these 6 rows once.
Row 66: (with C4) P4, (with C3) P to end of row.
Row 67: (with C3) K to last 4 st. (with C4) K4.
Row 68: (with C4) P8, (with C1) P to end of row.
Row 69: (with C1) K to last 8 st. (with C4) K8.
Row 70: (with C4) P12, (with C1) P to end of row.
Row 71: (with C1) K to last 12 st. (with C4) K12.
Row 72: (with C4) P16, (with C1),P to end of row.
Row 73: (with C1) K to last 16 st. (with C4) K16.
Row 74: (with C4) P20, (with C1) P to end of row.
Row 75: (with C1) K to the last 20, (with C4) K20.
Row 76: (with C4) P24, (with C1) P to end of row.
Row 77: (with C1) K to last 24, (with C4) K 24.

93

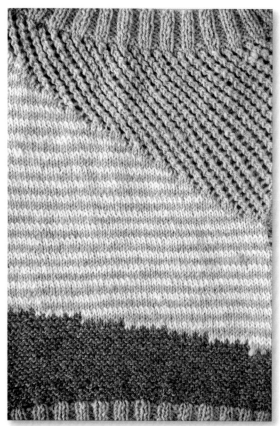

stitches and knit the side panels. Sew these knitted side panels to the back panel and sew the shoulder seams.

Sleeves:
The sleeves are knit separately and sewn onto the front and back panels afterwards.

Cast on 5 st.

Row 1: K

Row 2: P

Row 3: M1, K to last stitch, M1 (M1, insert your needle in the front and then in the back of the stitch, creating 2 stitches out of one.) Do this at the beginning and end of the knit side.

Repeat Row 2 and 3 until you have 37 st.

Next row: Cast on 6 st., K to end of row.

Next row: Cast on 6 st. and P to end of row.

Continue in this manner until all stitches are knit and purled with C4.

Then K and P in stockinette st. for 6 more rows.

Put all the stitches on stitch holders.

Repeat this for the back panel.

Side panels:
Using your front panel, with the right side facing you, pick up 36 st. from the bottom edge of the panel upwards to the arm opening.

With C3, K and P in stockinette st. for 4 inches, approx. 20 rows.

Bind off.

Repeat on the other side of the front panel. It is only from both sides of the front panel that you pick up

Next row: K

Next row: K6, P to last 6 st., K6.

Repeat these 2 rows 4 more times.

Now start to decrease.

Next row: *K6, K2 TOG, K to end of row.

Next row: K6, P2 TOG, P to last 6 st., K6.

Next row: K

Next row K6, P to last 6 st., K6*

Repeat these 4 rows until there are 36 st. left.

Change to needle size #6 and in K2, P2 rib pattern, knit
and purl for 1.5 more inches.

Bind off loosely.

Finishing:

Sew the sleeves to the front and the back panels.

Weave in all loose ends and gently block the sweater
in shape.

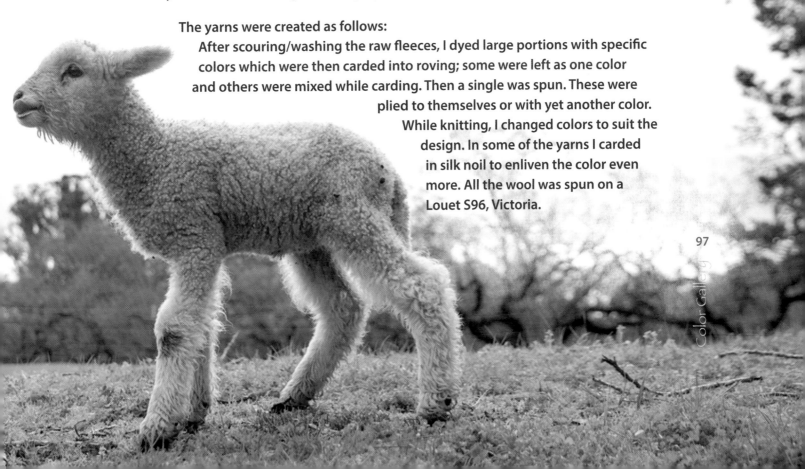

....

PART THREE

COLOR SECTION ~ GALLERY

Hand-spun , hand-dyed, color-carded and color-plyed

This section is more of a gallery for inspiration than a true knitters' pattern guide. The patterns are rough sketches to give the knitter and spinner inspiration and guidelines on how to make garments from your own hand-spun yarn.

All garments are made from local wool and alpaca and hand processed from raw fleece.

The designs and structure of the sweaters are fairly basic and designed in sections, so smaller individual skeins from one bobbin can be used. My bobbins hold approx. 250 to 350 yards of 2 ply, light worsted weight. As a hand spinner, the key challenge for a larger garment is to keep the size of the yarn the same throughout the project.

The yarns were created as follows:
After scouring/washing the raw fleeces, I dyed large portions with specific colors which were then carded into roving; some were left as one color and others were mixed while carding. Then a single was spun. These were plied to themselves or with yet another color. While knitting, I changed colors to suit the design. In some of the yarns I carded in silk noil to enliven the color even more. All the wool was spun on a Louet S96, Victoria.

97

Color Gallery

Echium Sweater

This sweater was inspired by the colors in Luxor, Egypt. Years ago, we stayed in an old mediterranean style hotel with white curtains in the tall hallways blowing in the wind against the periwinkle blue walls. Looking through the long hallways onto the Nile which had a different shade of blue with sailing boats in more white and blue hues was magical. Later, the echium plants in my garden had the same blue tones.

Skill level:
Easy to Intermediate

Measurements:
The size given fits a small to medium size person. Only one size is given at this time

Finished size:
Chest: 22"
Length to armhole: 13"
Armhole depth: 7"
Total Length: 20"
Sleeve length to underarm: 19.5"

Yarn:
7 skeins of light worsted 2 ply wool
Bo-Rage hand-spun local wool, hand dyed in roving, with commercial green dyes, color carded and color plied. Each skein is differently colored, but all colors work with each other.
Total yardage: approx. 1250 yards and approx. 400 grams or 15 oz.
Equivalent weight in a commercial yarn would be Cascade 220.

Needles:
Size # 6 needle for the body, or correct needles to obtain gauge. Main needle
Size # 4 needle for the bottom and sleeve bands

Notions:
Stitch holders
Embroidery needle
Measuring tape

Gauge:
3.5 st. = 1 inch
5.5 rows = 1 inch.

Color Gallery

up stitches. The sleeves are knit from shoulder to wrist from stitches picked up at the shoulder.

Back central panel: (8" wide)

Cast on 30 stitches with provisional cast on.
Knit first row.
Work in stockinette stitch pattern, (knit one row, purl one row) until piece measures 17.5 inches from the cast on edge.
Bind off.

Side back panels:

Pick up 70 st. along the side of the back panel.
With RS facing you, knit 2 rows so the second row will make a decorative ridge on the RS.
Then start stockinette stitch.
Next 2 rows, knit and purl in stockinette stitch inserting another color every 3 st. So, K2 with C1, K1 with C2.
Purl the next row in color format.
After 4 rows, use a different color and continue knitting and purling changing color/yarns several times, until you reach 6 inches from your picked up stitches of the central panel.
Bind off.
Repeat this on the other side of the back panel.

Front central panel:

Cast on 30 stitches with provisional cast on.
Knit first row.
Work in stockinette stitch pattern (knit one row, purl one row) until piece measures 10.5" from the cast on edge.
Bind off.

Side front panels:

Pick up 34 st., then cast on 36 st. (70 in total). The cast on stitches form your neck opening.
Knit first 2 rows to create a decorative ridge, and then continue with stockinette stitch.
Change color and continue with stockinette stitch.
Continue changing color a few times until you reach 6"

Stitch pattern:

Stockinette stitch
The borders are knit in K2, P2 rib pattern.

General note:

The sweater is knit in sections. The front and the back have central panels from which stitches are picked up and knit sideways. Then the collar is knit from picked up stitches, and the bottom band is knit from picked

ECHIUM SWEATER

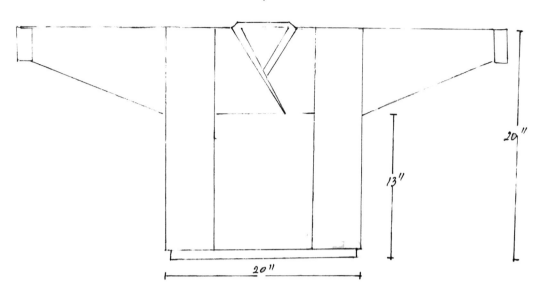

from pick up row of the central panel.
Bind off.

Do the same on the other side of the
front central panel.

Sew front and back together leaving
opening of approx. 7" for the
sleeves.

Sleeves:

Pick up 60 st. around the armhole
(30 st. on the front and 30 st. on the
back side).

Knit and purl in stockinette stitch pattern for 3", then start the decreases.
Decrease the 4th stitch at each end
of the the row. (K3, K2 TOG at the
beginning of your row and SSK, K3 at
the end of your row) every 4 rows.
Continue in this manner until you
reach approx. 14", then decrease every 2 rows until you have 32 st. left.

Continue in pattern until you
have 17". Change color and
needle size and do the cuff in
K2, P2 rib pattern for 2.5 more
inches.
Bind off.

Collar:

Pick up 90 stitches along the
side front panels and top of
back panel, and knit and purl
in stockinette stitch for 9".
Bind off.

Overlap the front flaps and
sew them to the top of the
front panel.

Finishing:

Weave in all loose ends.
Block and shape with warm
iron.

Lairds Landing Cardigan

Lairds Landing was the home of Clayton Lewis, a fisherman and watercolorist who sent his mother a hand-painted postcard each day of the year. He lived off the grid on the shore of Tomales Bay and would row his boat to the hamlet of Tomales to post his postcards, which were in rich saturated blues. The blue and green yarns I had hand-spun looked beautiful together and reminded me of Clayton's work. The Entrelac stitch pattern is a perfect way to highlight colors and make your yarn look like brushstrokes from a painter's palette.

Skill level:
Experienced

This pattern assumes that you know the Entrelac stitch pattern.
To understand Entrelac, I recommend that you go to Prescilla Gibsen-Roberts' book "Knitting in the Old Way". She has an extensive and very clear section on Entrelac knitting.

Measurements:
This cardigan fits a medium to large person. Only one size is given.

Finished size:
Total Length: 22"
Length, bottom to armhole: 12"
Armhole Length: 10"
Right Front width: 11"
Sleeve length: 20"
Back Width: 16 "
Bottom band: 2"

Yarn:
Bo-Rage hand-spun, 2 ply DK weight. All colors were hand-dyed, color-carded and color-plyed. Total yarn weight approx. 15 OZ. and approx. 1500 yards.
The sample is knit with 6 different variegated colors.
Equivalent commercial yarn could be Malabrigo worsted weight.

Needles:
Size #6: or correct needle size to obtain gauge. Main needle
Size #4 (36") circular needle for borders

Notions:
Embroidery needle
Stitch markers
Stitch holders
Tape measure

Gauge:
4 st. = 1 Inch
6 rows = 1 inch

Stitch pattern:
Entrelac for front and back panels
Stockinette for side panels and sleeves
Rib pattern (K2, P2) for borders

General note:
For the spinners.
This cardigan is designed and ideal for using hand-spun skeins of wool. Usually one bobbin has between 250/350 yards and 2.5 oz. to 3.5 oz. I have used 5 colors for the back and 4 for the front Entrelac section of the cardigan with a sixth color for the sides and border bands.

The yarn was dyed in roving and color-carded with silk noil in some skeins. I usually dye a large quantity of main color and then card, spin and ply with other colors. Having one main color makes it easier to maintain the same tonality within all the various variegated colors.

For the knitters:
The construction of this cardigan is rather straightforward, but it is done in a particular sequence. The back is one large rectangle, knit sideways, as are the front panels. The sides of the front decrease for the armholes. The arms are straight stockinette. The border bands are picked up afterwards and knit in K2, P2 ribbing. You need to pick up and work the bottom border of the fronts and back, before you work the front button bands.

When I refer to "block rows" I mean one row of Entrelac squares or triangles. The squares consist of 10 rows and 10 stitches each; these are worked in a row of blocks before you start the next row of blocks.

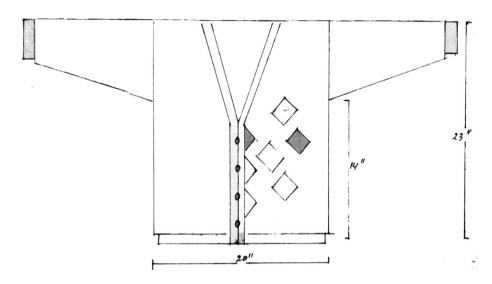

LAIRD'S LANDING SWEATER

Colors used:

C1 = Variegated dark blues plied with white
C2 = Variegated light greens
C3 = Variegated dark greens
C4 = Variegated light blues
C5 = Variegated blues/browns
C6 = Variegated blues/reds/purples

Back:

Knit a rectangle sideways without decreasing for the sleeves. Before you start the Entrelac pattern, knit and purl in Stockinette st. as described below.
Each Entrelac square or triangle is 10 st. and 10 rows.

Cast on 60 st.
Knit and purl in Stockinette st. for 2". (approx.14 rows) with C1.
After 2" start the Entrelac triangles with C2.
After your first row of triangles, with C3, knit in Entrelac a block row of squares.
With every Entrelac block row, you change colors.
After 5 block rows of squares, do another block row of triangles.

With C6, K and P 14 more rows in stockinette stitch. You should have approx. 12" of Entrelac, and 4" (2" each side) of stockinette. Total piece should measure 16" wide and 20" long.

Front and side panels:

Knit sideways from the underside of the sleeve to the front.
Start with an underarm panel of stockinette st., then knit in Entrelac and end with the button band (after you finish the bottom band).

Cast on 40 St. with C6.
Knit and purl in stockinette st. for 4" (approx. 24 rows). This is the underarm section.
Cast on 20 more st. for the front side (60 st.).
K these 20 st, turn and purl back to the bottom of the panel (top of the panel for the left side).
Now start with the Entrelac st. with C4.
Start with a block row of triangles and follow with 3 block rows of squares and another block row of triangles.
K and P 4 more rows in stockinette with C6.

Leave all 60 st. live on a stitch holder.

Right and left front bottom bands:

Pick up 42 st. each side. With RS facing you K 1 row with C5.

Next 2 rows, work in K2, P2 rib stitch format. Change color (to C6) and continue in rib pattern for 7 more rows.

Bind off.

Back bottom band:

Pick up 64 st. and repeat directions for the right and left front bottom bands.

Next you have a choice.

You can sew the shoulders together, Entrelac against Entrelac, which is not the best seam. Or you can pick up the shoulder stitches and knit and purl (stockinette st.) 2 rows on the back and the front panels to get a more pleasing worked off shoulder seam.

Front button bands:

Pick up all the "live" sts on your 2 fronts (140 total, 70 each side including the 10 extra st at the bottom band) AND pick up approx. 20 st. on the back. (160 total) onto the #4, 36" circular needle.

Knit and purl in stockinette st. for 3 rows with C5.

Change color to C6, K2 and P2 in rib st. for 2 rows.

Start the right bottom part of the band where the buttons are. This is wider than the top of the band.

Row 6: With RS facing you and at the right front bottom, K2, P2, 30 st. Turn.

Row 7: K2, P2 back to bottom.

Row 8: K2, P2 to end of row (to the bottom of the left front panel) [This is the row where you make the button holes].

Row 9: K2, P2 30 st. Turn (Left right front).

Row 10: K2 , P2 back to bottom.

Row 11: K2, P2 all st. (to the bottom the right front panel) [In this row you finish the button holes].

Row 12: K2, P2 30 st. Turn.

Row 13: K2, P2 back to the bottom.

Row 14: Bind off 130 st. K2 and P2 last 30 st.

Row 15: K2, P2 30 st.

Row 16: Bind off remaining 30 st.

Sleeves:
Pick up 70 st. at shoulder.
Knit and purl in Stockinette st. from shoulder to wrist.
Shape the sleeves by decreasing 1 st. each side every
4 rows. When there are 46 st left, work straight until
you have the correct length of the sleeve (approx. 18").
Finish with a K2, P2 rib band of approx. 2 inches.
Bind off.

Tip:
To color coordinate the sleeves, split in half every ball
of yarn left over and use the colors at random. For the
wrist band use C6, the same color as that of the button
and bottom bands

Finishing:
Weave in all loose ends and gently block the cardigan.

Rage Yarns

Surfer's Beanie

West Marin and specifically Bolinas is known for its surf. The water is cold but the surf is gentle and perfect for beginners. When getting out of the water dripping wet, a hat or beanie to warm your head is perfect. That is why I created this beanie.

Skill level:
Easy

Measurements:
15" diameter at head band
8" from bottom band to top

Yarn:
Bo-Rage hand-spun 2 ply, DK weight, various colors
Total approx. 200 yards. approx. 1.5 oz..
C1 = variegated dark blue approx. 100 yards
C2 = Variegated brown and lilac approx. 70 yards
C3 = Yellow approx. 10 yards
C4 = Lime green approx. 10 yards
C5 = Dark pink approx. 10 yards
Equivalent commercial yarn would be Cascade 220

Needles:
Circular 24" #4 for body of hat or needle size to obtain gauge. Main needle
Circular 24" #3 for the band
Double pointed needles #4

Notions:
Stitch marker
Measuring tape
Embroidery needle

Gauge:
5.5 st. = 1 inch
8 rows = 1 inch

Stitch pattern:
Stockinette st. (Knit all rows because you are knitting circular.)
Rib pattern for the band (K2,P2)

General note:
Cast on stitches and make sure they are not twisted when you bring the first and last stitch together. The color changes are easily made by stranding. There are never more than two colors used at the same time. The yarn itself has color variations as well.

Band:
With needle size #3 and with C2, cast on 90 st. Place marker at the beginning of your row.
In rib pattern (K2, P2) knit and purl for 2 rows.
Change to color C1 and knit and purl in rib pattern for 14 more rows, approx. 2".

Body of the hat:
With needle size #4 and with C3 knit one row and purl one row. (This will give you a ridge.)
Change color to C1 and knit 4 rows.
Next row: K2 st. with C1 and K2 st. with C4, alternating, for 2 rows.
Next knit 10 rows with C1.
Next row: K2 with C5 and K2 with C1, alternating, for 2 rows.
Next knit 10 rows with C1.
Next row: K2 with C4 and K2 with C2, alternating, for 2 rows.

Crown:
Now the decreases start and at some point double pointed needles will be easier.
Next row: With C2, *K2 TOG, K10*, repeat to end of row.
Next row: K
Next row: *K2 TOG, K9*, repeat to end of row.
Next row: K
Continue in this manner until you have 40 st. left.
Next row: K2 with C2 and K2 with C4, alternating.
Continue with the decreases until you have 6 st. left.
Break thread and with the embroidery needle pull thread through the 6 loops.
Pull tight and weave end through the wrong side of the top.

Finishing:
Weave in all loose ends into the wrong side of the hat.

Limantour Sweater

Limantour is a wide open sandy beach, sun drenched and full of light. All colors are slightly bleached because of the brightness of the sun and the light bouncing off the wide, white sandy beach. In this environment all the colors blend into one overall hue, giving a feeling of pure summer delight.

Skill level:
Easy to Intermediate

Measurements:
This sweater fits a small to medium person. Only one size is given.

Finished size:
Top to bottom: 20"
Bottom to underarm: 12"
Width: 20"

Yarn:
Bo-Rage hand-spun, 2 ply light worsted weight, color-carded and color-plied. All colors are variegated. Approx. 1300 yards, 13 oz.
C1 is a light blue
C2 is a yellow
C3 is a ochre
C4 is a darker blue
Equivalent commercial yarn would be Cascade 220.

Needles:
Circular needle size #6 for body or needle size to obtain gauge. Main needle Circular size #4 for bottom and sleeve bands

Notions:
Stitch markers
Tape measure

Gauge:
4 st. = 1 inch
6 rows = 1 inch

General note:
This sweater is knit in stockinette stitch and in panels: front panel and back panel.
Then stitches are picked up at the side of these panels and knit sideways. The sleeves are knit from the shoulder to the wrist from stitches picked up at the shoulder. The sleeve and bottom bands are knit in K2, P2 rib pattern afterwards. Back and front central panels are identical.
You knit with two colors at a time, never more than two colors.

111

Color Gallery

and purl 4 rows with C1.

Row 11: K2 with C1 and K2 with C2 (strand the 2nd color), alternating.

Row 12: Next row purl all stitches in color pattern.

Row 13: Repeat row 11.

Row 14: Repeat row 12.

Row 15 - 18: K and purl with C1.

Row 19: K4 with C1, K4 with C2, alterna ing.

Row 20: Purl all stitches in color pattern.

Row 21: Repeat row 19.

Row 22 Repeat row 20.

Row 23 - 26: K and P with C1.

Repeat these eight rows (row 19 - row 26) until you have 18".

Bind off.

Side front and side back panels:

Pick up 80 st. along the side of the front (or back) panel and knit and purl in stockinette stitch with C3 for 4.5 inches.

Bind off.

Do the same for the other side.

Sew the front and back together at the shoulders, leaving 10" for the neck opening and 8" for the sleeves.

Sleeves:

Pick up 60 st. with circular needle and knit back and forth (not in the round). A circular needle makes it easier.

Knit and purl in stockinette st. for 6 rows, then start the decreases.

Decrease 1 st. each side of the needle every 4 rows. For a more pleasing finish, decrease the 3rd stitch on each side by K2 TOG and SSK). When you have 40 st. left, continue in stockinette stitch until you reach 13". Change to needle size #4 and in rib pattern (K2, P2) work two more inches for the band.

Bind off.

Back and front central panel:

To get the variety of color, change color either for the background or for the squares every eight rows.

With needle size #6 and C1, provisionally CO 48 st. Knit and purl in stockinette st. for 10 rows, approx. 1.5 inches. Then introduce C2.

Next, knit and purl 4 rows with 2 colors and then knit

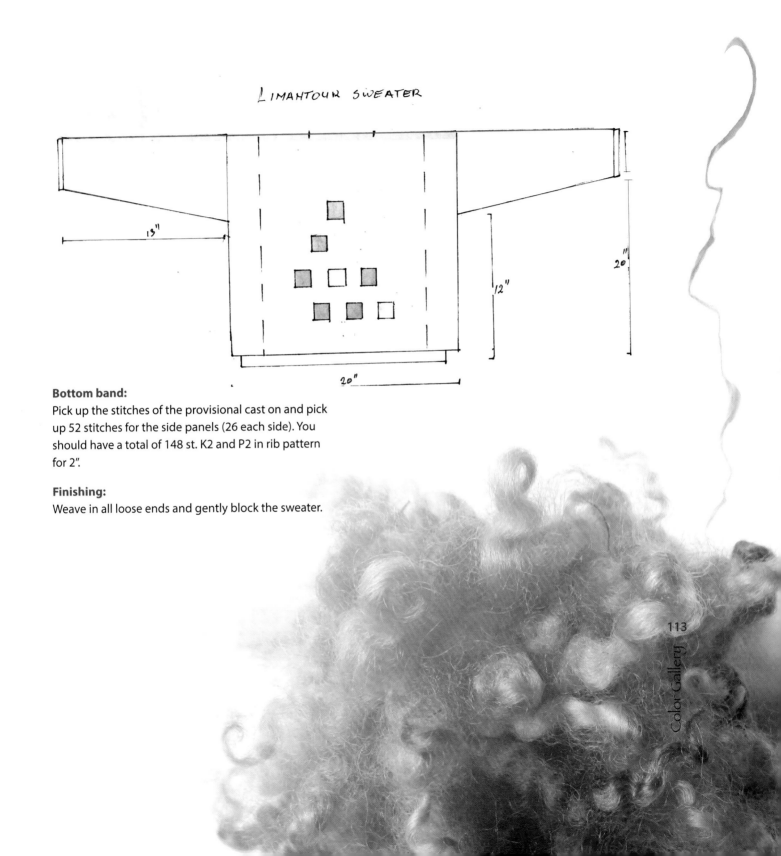

LIMAHTOUR SWEATER

Bottom band:

Pick up the stitches of the provisional cast on and pick up 52 stitches for the side panels (26 each side). You should have a total of 148 st. K2 and P2 in rib pattern for 2".

Finishing:

Weave in all loose ends and gently block the sweater.

Audubon Canyon Cardigan

Audubon Canyon has long winding walking trails that take you through darker redwood groves and fern-filled stream-beds. The fall colors in the canyons are dark grey and red browns. The inspiration for this cardigan came from Ann's beautiful hand-spun yarn under her label Feline Fibers. She is one of the best spinners I know. Ann is a shearer of alpacas and llamas and travels up and down the West Coast at shearing time.

Skill level:
Intermediate

Measurements:
The size of this cardigan is a medium. Only one size is given.

Finished size:
Total length: 21"
Bottom to under sleeve: 11.5"
Width: 18"
Sleeve length: 20"
Collar width: 1"
Bottom band width: 2"

Yarn:
Bo-Rage mill spun 2 ply, heavy worsted weight. (grey)

Feline Fibers 2 ply hand-spun, heavy worsted weight (browns)
Approx. 800 yards, 16 oz. for the mill-spun grey
Approx. 600 yards, 12 oz for the hand-spun brown
Equivalent commercial yarns would be Brown Sheep, Lamb's Pride worsted weight
Colors:
C1 is mill-spun - grey
C2 is Ann's Feline Fibers hand-spun - brown

Needles:
Needle size #8 for body or needle size to obtain gauge Main needle
Needle size #6 for borders

Notions:
Tapestry needle
Tape measure
Buttons

Gauge:
4 st. = 1 inch
5.5 rows = 1 inch

Stitch pattern:

Stockinette st. for the body

Rib Stitch (K2,P2) for the border bands

General note:

This cardigan is knit from the bottom to the top. It is a fairly common construction. The sleeves are set in at a right angle. The front button band is knit afterwards from picked up stitches. The wrist bands, bottom bands and front button bands are worked off by using the colored hand-spun as the final bind off row.

Back:

Cast on 70 st. with a provisional cast on.

K2 with C1, K2 with C2, alternating. Repeat to end of row.

Purl back in color pattern.

Switch color positions. *K2 with C2, K2 with C1*, alternating. Repeat to end of row.

Purl back in color pattern.

Knit two rows C2.

Knit in color pattern until you reach 11.5", then decrease for sleeves.

Decrease 6 st. each side.

Continue to knit in color patterns until you reach 18". Bind off.

Front:

Cast on 40 st. with a provisional cast on.

K2 with C1 and K2 with C2 to the end of the row. Purl back in color pattern.

Repeat these two rows.

Row 5: K2 with C2 and k2 with C1, alternating, to the end of the row. Purl back in color pattern.

Repeat these 2 rows.

Next knit and purl 6 rows with C2.

Next row K4 with C1, K4 with C2, alternating, to end of row. Purl back in color pattern.

Repeat these two rows one more time.

Next knit and purl 4 rows with C1.

Next *K4 with C1 and K4 with C2*, alternating. Repeat to end of row. Purl back in color pattern.

Repeat these two rows one more time.

K and purl four rows with C1.

K and purl four rows with C2.

Next *K4 with C1 and K4 with C2*, alternating. Repeat to end of row. Purl back in color pattern.

Repeat these two rows one more time.

Next *K1 with C2, K4 with C1*, alternating. Repeat to end of row. Purl back in color pattern.

Next row *K1 with C1, K4 with C2*, alternating. Repeat to end of row. Purl back in color pattern.

Next row *K1 with C2, K with C1*, alternating. Repeat to end of row. Purl back in color pattern.

*Knit 4 rows with C1.

Next row K4 with C2, K4 with C2, alternating. Repeat to end of row. Purl back in color pattern.

Repeat these last two rows one more time.

Now decrease for sleeves:

Bind off 8 st.

Repeat color pattern from * to * until you reach 15".

Now you decrease for the neck opening:

Bind off 8 st.

Continue in pattern until you reach 18".

Bind off.

Sleeves:

Knit from the shoulder to the wrists using chart 2 color pattern for sleeves.

Pick up 74 st.

Knit and purl 10 rows in stockinette st.

Decrease 1 st. each side every 4 rows until you have 40 st. left, then stop with the decreases.

Knit and purl in stockinette st. until you reach 17".

With needle size #6 work 3 more inches in rib pattern (K2, P2).

Switch to C2.

Bind off.

Bottom band:

Next sew shoulders and side and sleeves together.

With needle #6, pick up the provisional cast-on stitches at the bottom of the cardigan and knit and purl in rib pattern (K2, P2) for two inches.

Bind off.

Button band:

Pick up 76 st. from the front panels.

With C1, knit and purl in stocki-

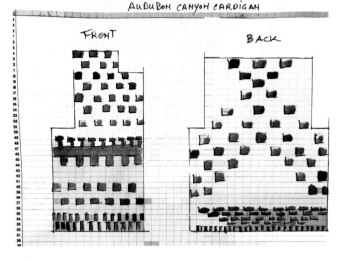

AUDUBON CANYON CARDIGAN

FRONT   BACK

nette st. 4 rows.

Change to C2, knit and purl 2 rows

Change to C1 and needle size #6.

In rib pattern (K2, P2) work 4 rows.

Next create button holes and continue in rib pattern for 12 rows.

Change to C2 and bind off.

Repeat this for the other side without the button holes.

Neck band:

With needles size #6, pick up 72 st.

With C2 knit and purl 2 rows in stockinette st.

Change to C1 and in rib pattern (K2, P2) work 6 rows. Change to C2 and bind off.

To shape the neckline, while working the neck band, decrease 1 st. at the corners, approx. 14 st. at the beginning and 14 st. at the end of your row, every other row.

Finishing:

Weave in all loose ends and gently block the cardigan.

Woolscapes

Bear Valley Sweater

Bear Valley is the focal point of Point Reyes National Seashore with a most pleasant and moderate walk to the ocean to view the spectacular yellow sunsets against the dark blue sea and lighter blue skies.

Skill level:
Intermediate

Measurements:
This sweater fits a small to medium size person. It is cropped short.

Finished size:
Top to bottom: 19"
Armhole depth: 8"
Bottom width: 19"
Sleeve length to underarm: 18"

Yarn:
Bo-Rage hand-spun, hand dyed 2 ply. DK weight
Approx. 12 oz
Approx. 1200 Yards
Equivalent commercial yarns would be Malabrigo, sports weight.

Needles:
Needle size # 6 or correct needle size to obtain gauge. Main needle
Needle size #4 for the borders

Notions:
Stitch holders
Embroidery needle
Measuring tape

Gauge:
5 st. = 1 inch
8 rows = 1 inch

Stitch pattern:
Stockinette
Rib Pattern (P2, K2) for bottom and wrist bands

General note:
This sweater is knit in panels. Three panels for the back and three panels for the front, plus the sleeves. Start with the center back panel, then pick up stitches along the side of the center panel and knit to the desired width and repeat on the other side of the center back panel.

Color Gallery

at the bottom to light at the top, from light at the center to darker under the arm. Sleeves are dark at the top and light at the wrists. However, all colors can be used at will, disregarding all rules.

Back center panel:
Cast on 20 stitches with provisional cast on. Knit and purl in stockinette stitch until you have 17".
Bind off.
Change color from dark at the bottom to light at the top.

Back side panels:
Pick up 80 stitches on the side of the panel and knit 7" sideways.
Bind off.
Do the same on the other side of the center panel.

Front left panel:
For the left front panel cast on 60st. with the provisional cast on method.
Knit and purl (stockinette st.) 2 rows, then start the decreases. Decrease only on the left side of the panel.
Decrease 1 st. every 2 rows.
You should have 26 st. left at 14". Then you increase on the same side you decreased, increasing 1 st. every 2 rows. for 2.5".
Bind off at 16.5". (approx. 27 rows)

Front "wedge" panel:
Pick up 50 st. at the diagonal part of the front left panel. These stitches should measure approx. 10" (measured diagonally), or (9" measured straight up and down from the bottom)
You are knitting sideways with the short rows at the top of the picked up stitches. Knit and purl these short rows in stockinette st. until you reach a length of 4.5" at the top and .5" at the bottom.

For the front, the left side panel is knit first, diagonal on one side. Then stitches are picked up and knit sideways with short rows to create the "wedge". The right front side panel is knit separately. The sleeves are knit from picked up stitches at the shoulder and knit towards the wrists. Then all bottom stitches are picked up and the bottom band is knit down. The neck is worked off by crocheting a band around it.

Color work:
As you can see in the sample, the colors go from dark

BEAR VALLEY SWEATER

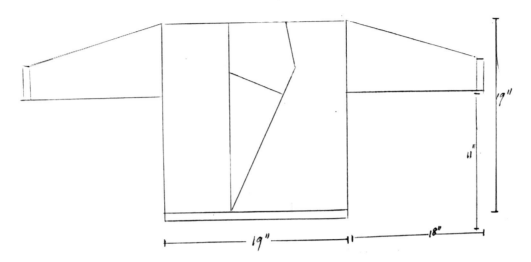

19"
11"
19"
18"

Continue with the front right panel.
When you reach the 4.5", increase 30 more st. until you have 80 st. The increases should be at the top of the panel. They form the neck opening and will be the shoulder part of the front. Knit and purl in stockinette st. changing colors as you go, for 6 more inches.
Bind off.

Sew front and back panel together at the shoulders and on the sides leaving opening for the sleeves.

Sleeves:
At the shoulder pick up 60 st around the arm opening for the sleeve and start knitting down.
After 10 rows of stockinette st., decrease 1 st. each side every 4 rows, until you have 40 st. left on your needles. Work in stockinette st. until you reach 16".
Change to your border color and to your border needle size and in rib pattern (k2, p2) work for 2 more inches.

Finishing:
Pick up 180 stitches at the bottom of the sweater and in rib pattern (K2, P2) work for 2 more inches to finish

the border band of the sweater. With your border color, crochet around the neck line, accentuating the irregular shape. Weave in all the loose ends and block.

Summer Ocean Top

The inspiration for this top was long horizons of pale and dark blue ocean water with a light blue sky and relaxing on the beach during the yellow and orange sunsets.

Skill level:
Easy

Measurements:
This sweater fits a small to medium size person. It is a short cropped, sleeveless sweater.

Finished size:
Top to bottom: 15"
Armhole depth: 7"
Bottom width: 23"
Central panels: 10"
Side panels: 6.5 "

Yarn:
Bo-Rage hand-spun , hand-dyed 2 ply, DK weight
Approx. 9 oz
Approx. 900 Yards
Equivalent commercial yarn would be Cascade 220

Needles:
US size #4 and US size #6, main needle or correct needles to obtain gauge

Notions:
Stitch holders
Embroidery needle
Measuring tape
Crochet hook (size H)

Gauge:
4 st. = 1 inch
6 rows = 1 inch

Stitch pattern:
Stockinette

General note:
This sweater is knit in panels, three panels for the back and three panels for the front. Front and back are the same construction.

Start with the center back panel, then pick up stitches along the side of the center panel and knit sideways for approx. 6.5 inches and repeat with the other side of the center back panel. The total width should be approx. 23 inches.

Color Gallery

Front and back central panels:

With a provisional cast on, CO 44 st. Knit and purl in stockinette st. for 14". Bind off.
As you are working, change colors to create the bands of color.

Side panels:

Pick up 50 st. and knit and purl in stockinette st. sideways for approx. 6.5 inches.
Bind off.

Do the same on the other side of the central panel.

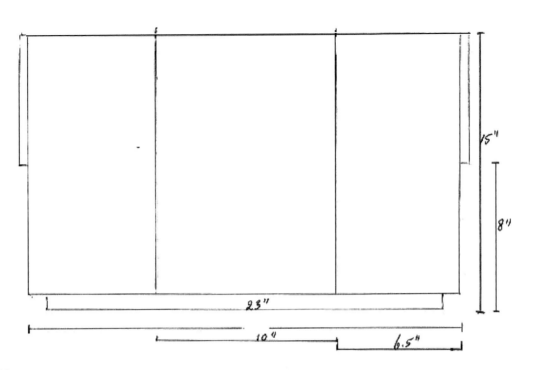

Finishing:

Pick up stitches at the bottom of the sweater and in
K2, P2 rib pattern work for 2".

With a crochet hook, crochet one row around the
edges of the neck and the arm openings.

Weave in all loose ends and gently block the sweater.

Abbreviations:

BO = Bind Off
C = color
C or CN = Cable needle
CIP = Continue in pattern
CO = Cast on
K = Knit
K2 tog = Knit two stitches together
KW = Knit wise
LH = Left hand
M1 = Make one = Knit in the front and back the same stitch
MN = Main needle
P = Purl
P2 tog = Purl two stitches together
PM = Place marker
Provisional BO = Provisional bind off
Provisional CO = Provisional cast on
PSSO = Pass slipped stitch over.
PU = Pick up
PW = Purl wise
RH = Right hand
Rib or R = Rib pattern
RS = Right side of the p piece
R = Rib stitch pattern (K2,P2) in Plowline pattern
St. = Stitch
Sts = Stitches
St. St. = Stockinette stitch.
S or Seed = Knit in seed pattern
S = Slip stitch in Plowline pattern
Sl = Slip stitch
SSK = Slip, slip, knit the two slipped stitches together
SSP = Slip, slip, purl the two slipped stitches together
St. St. = Stockinette stitch
wrpt or W&T = wrap & turn used when making "short rows"
WS = Wrong side of the piece
YO = yarn over
KFB = knit in the front and the back of the same stitch to create an increase
M1 = knit in the front and the back of the same stitch to create an increase
C2F = K1 onto cn and hold in front, P1, K1 from cn
C2B = P1 onto cn and hold in back, K1, P1 from cn
TSL = K1 onto cn hold in front, P1, K1 fron cn. = traveling stitch slanting left
TSR = P1 onto cn, hold in back, K1, P1 from cn. = traveling stitch slanting right
C3B#2 = K1 onto cn and hold in back of work, K2, K1 from cn
C3F#2 = K2 onto cn and hold in front of work, K1, K2 from the cn
C3B#1 = P1 onto cn and hold in back, K2, P1 from cn
C3F#1 = K2 onto cn and hold in front, P1, K2 from cn
C3BP = P2 onto cn and hold in back, K1, P2 from cn

C3FK = K1 onto cn and hold in front, P2, K1 from cn
C4B = K2 and place onto the cn and hold cn in back of work, K2 and then knit the 2 sts from cn
C4F = K2 and place onto the cn and hold in front of work, K2 and then knit the 2 sts from cn
C4PB = P2 onto cn and hold in back, K2, P2 from cn (left slant)
C4KF = K2 onto cn, hold in front, P2, K2 from cn (right slant)
TSRP = P1 onto CN and hold in back, K1, P1 from CN. Left slant
TSLP = K1 onto CN and hold in front, P1, K1 from CN. Right slant
TSR = K1 onto CN and hold in back, K1, k1 from cn (traveling st. right)
TSL = K1 onto CN and hold in front, K1, k1 from cn (traveling st. left)
TSP = Traveling stitch pattern
Rib pattern: In most cases the rib pattern used is K2, P2, repeated for a number of rows. In the pattern it is indicated how many stitches are knit and how many are purled
Short Rows/Wrap & Turn
When doing short rows, before turning piece to knit back in the other direction, complete the wrpt. as follows: Bring working yarn to the front, slip next stitch from left needle over to right needle, bring working yarn to the back, then slip stitch from right needle back to left needle, then turn.

Seed Stitch:
K1, P1. If the row ends on a purl stitch, you start the next row with a purl stitch. A purl stitch sits on top of a knit stitch.

Stockinette Stitch:
Knit one row and purl one row. Usually the knit (flat) side of the garment is the RS (right side).

Garter stitch:
Knit every row.

Stranding:
Carry one of the colors behind the main visible color by means of floats. When the floats get too big, you can secure the float by means of wrapping it (or securing it) with the main color. This is most easily done by holding a yarn in each hand when working with two colors.

Knitted Cast-on Method:
This is an excellent way to CO when you need to CO sts in continuation of a row. Hold the knitted piece in your left hand and the free needle in your right hand.
Place right hand needle into the last stitch of the row, and knit the stitch. Place the new twisted st on the left needle. Then, knit into the twisted stitch on the left hand needle, and again place it on left needle. You have now CO two stitches. Continue in this manner until you have added (CO) the number of stitches required.

Woolscapes

Sources:

The wool for both the Fibershed and hand-spun sweaters were sourced from farms usually less than thirty miles from my home. Over the years I have made friendships with these farmers, and they sometimes save fleeces for me with certain characteristics that they know I would love. They call me when shearing day happens so I can be there to have first choice and help with the skirting process.

Most Bo-Rage mill-spun and hand-spun yarns are available at my store:
Black Mountain Artisans
11245 Main Street, P.O. Box 586
Point Reyes Station, CA. 94956
bma@sonic.net
blackmountainartisans.com
online store: borageyarn.com and fibershedmarket-place.com

Fiber Farms

Mimi Luebbermann
Windrush Farm in Petaluma, West Marin County
Windrushfarmwool.com
Mimi has Corriedale/Finn crosses, a mid-range fleece that is perfect for this type of yarn and sweaters. She also has a herd of single-coated Shetlands. These are soft, multi colored and very nice in the mill-spun yarns.

Martha Cant
Starbuck Station Wools in Valley Ford, West Marin County
Martha has Wensleydales and Cormos. She covers her sheep year around to keep the fleeces as clean as possible. Cormo fleeces are very soft. Sometime it is hard to get the lanolin out of the fleece, but it is certainly worth it. Spinning Cormo is very special, the tight crimp wool slides from your hand into a smooth very thin thread. Her Wensleydales have long open curls which I like to spin as curls (see Coastal Sweater.)

Sandy Wallace and her husband Michael
Alpacas of Marin in Nicasio, West Marin County
info@alpacasofmarin.com
Sandy and Michael own a Huacaya herd and a Suri herd which produce silky and soft alpaca
multi-colored fleeces that I incorporate into the mix for softness and shine.

Within the Fibershed, there are many other fiber farms with wonderful fleeces. These three are the closest to me and the ones I have used for this book's projects.

Mills

Ariana and Casey
Casari Wool Mill in Point Arena.
www.CasariRanch.com
Ariana and Casey just recently moved from Valley Ford in West Marin County to Point Arena. They have a large sheep farm and decided to create a mill to process their fleeces. Their specialty is bedding, and they have done wonderful roving for me.

Jane Deamer
Yolo Wool Mill in Yolo County
Yolowoolmill.com
Jane created all of the Bo-Rage mill spun yarns. This is the closest mill (eighty miles from my home) that creates yarn (other mills create only roving) and the only larger mill within this Fibershed.

Marlie de Swart

Marlie is a fiber and ceramic artist. She has been involved in creating fiber works from local sources since childhood. She grew up in Holland, graduated from the Sorbonne in Paris and Occidental College near Pasadena and met her husband at Art Center College of Design. Throughout her life she has been involved in fiber arts with commissions and installations in Los Angeles and Amsterdam and galleries representing her work throughout the world. Currently Marlie has a local fiberarts cooperative store, Black Mountain Artisans, in Point Reyes Station, California. Marlie lives in Bolinas, California, Coastal West Marin County.

Paige Green

Paige is a documentary and portrait photographer, in Petaluma, California, whose storytelling approach to photography frequently addresses issues involving agriculture, land use, and food. Her work is featured in eleven books and has been published in Glamour, National Geographic Traveler, New York Times Magazine, Conde Nast Traveler, GQ, Country Living, House Beautiful, and Culture.

A lover of natural light, medium format film, and capturing candid moments, Paige is excited by any photoshoot with kids, dogs, or good food (especially chocolate food) and she looks forward to spending the rest of her life capturing moments, photographing her family and documenting communities. Her philosophy in life and photography (and the tattoo she wants to get but never will)... Be Nice.

Barbara MacDonald

Test knitter and technical knitting advisor. Barbara has been a knitter most of her life. She is meticulous and applies a scientific and educational approach to writing patterns for fellow knitters. She is familiar with a variety of instructional methods and has advised on these projects in numerous ways. She has been a great source of inspiration and encouragement.